# The UK Air Fryer Cookbook 2023

## Easy and Affordable Recipes to Fry, Bake, Grill, Roast and Seafood, vegetables with Your Air Fryer

**Aimee Owen**

# Contents

# INTRODUCTION

The air fryer is a great tool on its own, but you can kick things up a notch when you use it with some other kitchen utensils you probably already have on hand. One of the dangers of air frying is overcooking the food you're making. With these tips, you'll avoid that problem and air fry like a pro! The air fryer obviously is a great way to prepare food in your kitchen, but have you ever thought about taking it on the road? With these tips, you'll be air frying wherever your wheels take you!

# 5 KITCHEN TOOLS TO USE WITH YOUR AIR FRYER

Nothing is worse than buying a new appliance that requires you to spend an extra hundred bucks in special gadgets, right? Rest assured, the air fryer does not require you to do that! Using those kitchen tools you already have on hand, your air-fried foods will come to life. And even if you're not a cook and you need to invest in a few of the items listed here, they won't cost you an arm and a leg and you'll find multiple uses for them in your home.

**Here are five air-fryer-friendly kitchen tools to have on hand:**

- Silicone muffin liners: Make your muffins come to life with silicone muffin liners. Heat stable and perfectly portioned, silicone muffin liners allow you to bring the beauty of breads to the comfort of your own kitchen. Plus, you can even make baked eggs in them.

- Seven-inch springform (Bundt) pan: Cheesecakes and coffee cakes have a seat at your table when you invest in one of these (usually sold as a convertible cake and Bundt cake pan). You can enjoy a bakery-fresh slice of cake for less than a fraction of the cost.

- Seven-inch oven-safe casserole dish: Most air fryers don't exceed 400 degrees, meaning the same small casserole dish that withstands your oven temperatures will be safe in your air fryer, too. From glass to metal to silicone, the air fryer should accommodate them all!

- Metal skewers: Take those skewers from the grill and use them in your air fryer to help evenly cook thicker cuts of meat. Depending on the type of air fryer you have, the skewers may (or may not) be too big for your fryer. If you're on the fence about skewers that will fit your air fryer, you can use wooden sticks (just be cautious of the temperature so you don't catch them on fire).

- Kitchen tongs: Using a pair of kitchen tongs is essential to ensure you don't burn another finger trying to get that last chip that's nestled itself on the side of the fryer basket.

# 5 WAYS TO PREVENT AIR FRYING YOUR FOOD TO A CRISP

When cooking certain foods at high temperatures, charring can occur. That charring produces a chemical called acrylamide. And acrylamide might be linked to an increased risk of cancer. It's important to note that, according to the American Cancer Society, "It's not yet clear if the levels of acrylamide in foods raise cancer risk." Still, **you can take some steps to avoid frying foods to a crisp. Here's what we recommend:**

- Cook at lower temperatures for longer periods of time (instead of high temperatures for shorter periods). Turning the temperature knob down to 300 to 325 degrees and increasing the time to 10 or 20 minutes may prevent charred coffee cake and blackened fries.

- Cover foods with foil. The air fryer works to cook your foods by circulating air throughout the basket, so you don't want to prevent that air flow. However, you can use foil to cover a chicken breast, for example, and place it in the basket to cook (low and slow). We also suggest using foil to cover cakes and egg dishes to prevent the top from cooking too quickly. Just be sure there is enough room between the foil and the top of the air fryer.

- Don't overfill the basket. You may be tempted to throw the entire batch of beet chips or broccoli florets into the basket at once to save time, but that will result in uneven cooking and a few pieces getting burned to a crisp. Either invest in a larger fryer or cook in smaller batches to produce the perfect air-fried foods every time.

- Use air-fryer-safe equipment. The key to producing bakery-perfect muffins or quick breads lies in making sure you're using the right equipment. Using the right equipment helps allow the air to circulate properly, leaving your air-fried foods crisp, crunchy, and evenly cooked.

- Set timers and reminders. We all need to set alarms to remember important things, and air frying your foods is no different. Set timers not only on your air fryer but on your phone so you don't leave the foods cooking any longer than required.

If you travel in an RV, you know space is tight. And yet many RVers are adding an air fryer to their tiny kitchens. Why? Because nothing beats an air fryer for reheating food with ease, making your favorite chicken wings without heating up your RV, and enjoying fresh baked cookies after a long day of hiking. But before you pack up, you need to understand the electrical requirements of both your vehicle and your air fryer, so be sure to review your camper's electrical needs first.

**When you've determined that your air fryer will work in your vehicle, you're ready to get cooking! The following simple meals will be perfect for your next road trip:**

- Chicken wings: This popular appetizer can be made in the comfort of your RV or camper in 22 minutes! Just season with salt and pepper and cook at 370 degrees for 22 minutes, flipping a couple times. Then finish off with your favorite hot sauce heated up with melted butter. Serve the wings with blue-cheese-stuffed celery, and call it a meal!

- Steak and potatoes: Who doesn't appreciate a good steak while taking in another stellar sunset? Dice potatoes and season with salt and pepper. Then cook at 360 degrees for 5 minutes. Season the steak with salt and pepper and place it in the air fryer basket next to the potatoes. Spray the food with cooking spray, crank up the heat to 390 degrees, and cook for 12 minutes, flipping the steak and shaking the potatoes after 6 minutes. Let the steak rest for 5 minutes, and serve with a simple salad to complete the meal.

- Crispy chimichangas: Whether it's for breakfast, lunch, or dinner, a chimichanga is an easy addition to your meal rotation. Try a simple bean and cheese chimichanga by spreading refried beans onto a tortilla, topping with shredded cheese, and rolling up like a sealed burrito. Spray the chimichanga with cooking spray and cook at 360 degrees for 8 to 10 minutes.

- BLT: Bacon comes out perfectly in an air fryer, without splattering grease all over your living space. Cook the bacon at 390 degrees for 8 to 10 minutes (or how you like it). Remove the bacon onto a paper towel. Then brush your bread with mayo and place it in the basket. Cook at 370 degrees for 2 minutes. Top with lettuce, tomato, and crispy bacon for a warm lunch!

- Frozen pizzas: Oh yes, that's right! You can now pick up your favorite frozen fare — from pizzas to Hot Pockets — at a grocery store instead of waiting in line at a restaurant. Be sure to pick up the individual sizes. Whip up a salad from a bag to complete the meal.

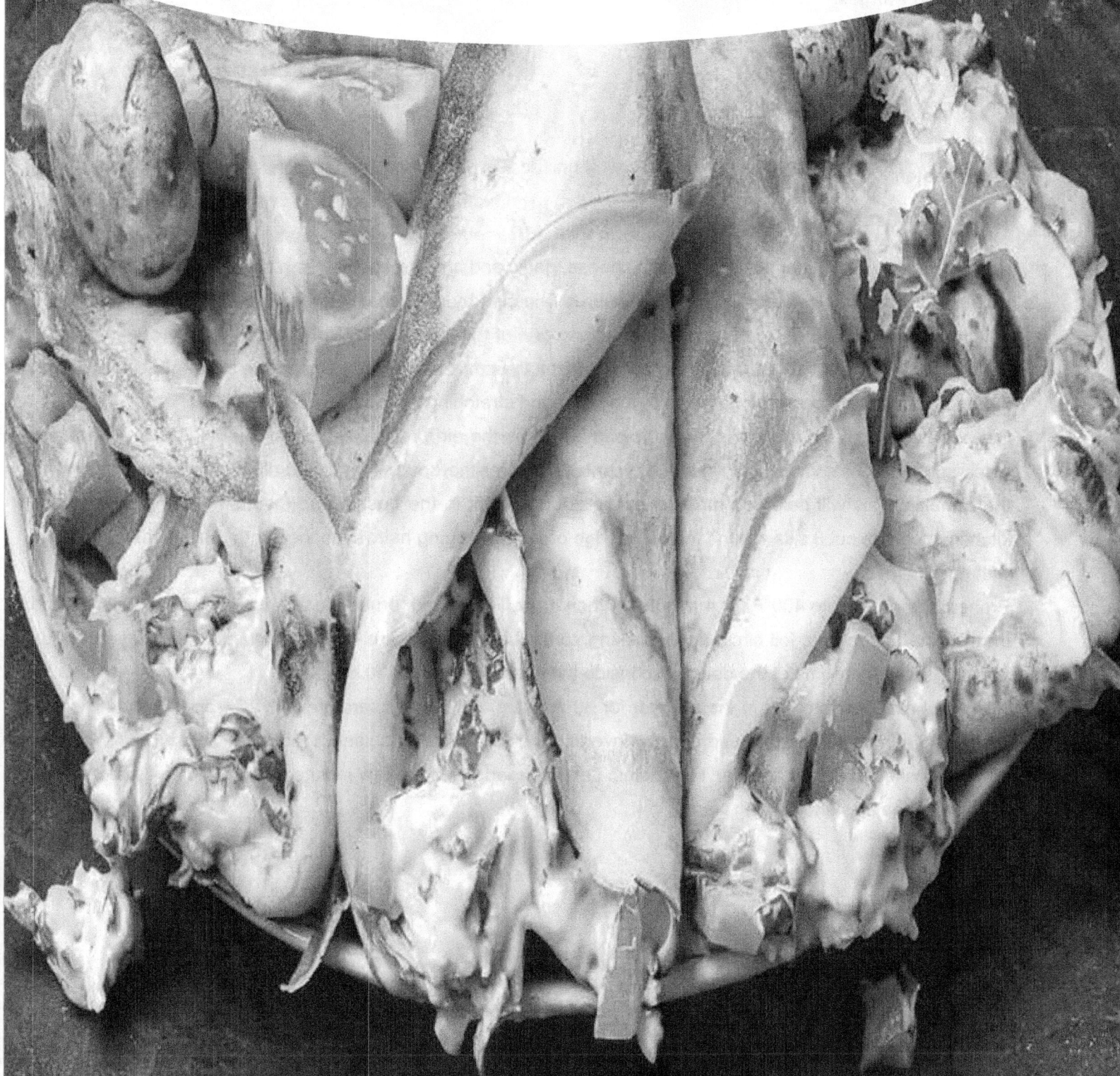

# BREAD AND BREAKFAST

# Apple-cinnamon-walnut Muffins

## Ingredients:

*Servings: 8*
*Cooking Time:*
*11 Mins.*

- 1 C. flour
- ⅓ C. sugar
- 1 tsp. baking powder
- ¼ tsp. baking soda
- ¼ tsp. salt
- 1 tsp. cinnamon
- ¼ tsp. ginger
- ¼ tsp. nutmeg
- 1 egg
- 2 tbsp. pancake syrup, plus 2 teaspoons
- 2 tbsp. melted butter, plus 2 teaspoons
- ¾ C. unsweetened applesauce
- ½ tsp. vanilla extract
- ¼ C. chopped walnuts
- ¼ C. diced apple
- 8 foil muffin cups, liners removed and sprayed with cooking spray

## Directions:

1. Preheat air fryer to 330°F.
2. In a large bowl, stir together flour, sugar, baking powder, baking soda, salt, cinnamon, ginger, and nutmeg.
3. In a small bowl, beat egg until frothy. Add syrup, butter, applesauce, and vanilla and mix well.
4. Pour egg mixture into dry ingredients and stir just until moistened.
5. Gently stir in nuts and diced apple.
6. Divide batter among the 8 muffin cups.
7. Place 4 muffin C. in air fryer basket and cook at 330°F for 11minutes.
8. Repeat with remaining 4 muffins or until toothpick inserted in center comes out clean.

# All-in-one Breakfast Toast

## Ingredients:

- 1 strip of bacon, diced
- 1 slice of 1-inch thick bread (such as Texas Toast or hand-sliced bread)
- 1 tbsp. softened butter (optional)
- 1 egg
- salt and freshly ground black pepper
- ¼ C. grated Colby or Jack cheese

## Directions:

1. Preheat the air fryer to 400°F.
2. Air-fry the bacon for 3 minutes, shaking the basket once or twice while it cooks. Remove the bacon to a paper towel lined plate and set aside.
3. Use a sharp paring knife to score a large circle in the middle of the slice of bread, cutting halfway through, but not all the way through to the cutting board. Press down on the circle in the center of the bread slice to create an indentation. If using, spread the softened butter on the edges and in the hole of the bread.
4. Transfer the slice of bread, hole side up, to the air fryer basket. Crack the egg into the center of the bread, and season with salt and pepper.
5. Air-fry at 380°F for 5 minutes. Sprinkle the grated cheese around the edges of the bread leaving the center of the yolk uncovered, and top with the cooked bacon. Press the cheese and bacon into the bread lightly to help anchor it to the bread and prevent it from blowing around in the air fryer.
6. Air-fry for one or two more minutes (depending on how you like your egg cooked), just to melt the cheese and finish cooking the egg. Serve immediately.

# Hole In One

## Ingredients:

- 1 slice bread
- 1 tsp. soft butter
- 1 egg
- salt and pepper
- 1 tbsp. shredded Cheddar cheese
- 2 tsp. diced ham

## Directions:

1. Place a 6 x 6-inch baking dish inside air fryer basket and preheat fryer to 330°F.
2. Using a 2½-inch-diameter biscuit cutter, cut a hole in center of bread slice.
3. Spread softened butter on both sides of bread.
4. Lay bread slice in baking dish and crack egg into the hole. Sprinkle egg with salt and pepper to taste.
5. Cook for 5minutes.
6. Turn toast over and top it with shredded cheese and diced ham.
7. Cook for 2 more minutes or until yolk is done to your liking.

# Sweet Potato-cinnamon Toast

## Ingredients:

- 1 small sweet potato, cut into ⅜-inch slices
- oil for misting
- ground cinnamon

## Directions:

1. Preheat air fryer to 390°F.
2. Spray both sides of sweet potato slices with oil. Sprinkle both sides with cinnamon to taste.
3. Place potato slices in air fryer basket in a single layer.
4. Cook for 4minutes, turn, and cook for 4 more minutes or until potato slices are barely fork tender.

# Seasoned Herbed Sourdough Croutons

## Ingredients:

- 4 C. cubed sourdough bread, 1-inch cubes (about 8 ounces)
- 1 tbsp. olive oil
- 1 tsp. fresh thyme leaves
- ¼ – ½ tsp. salt
- freshly ground black pepper

**Servings: 4**
**Cooking Time: 7 Mins.**

## Directions:

1. Combine all ingredients in a bowl and taste to make sure it is seasoned to your liking.
2. Preheat the air fryer to 400°F.
3. Toss the bread cubes into the air fryer and air-fry for 7 minutes, shaking the basket once or twice while they cook.
4. Serve warm or store in an airtight container.

# Southern Sweet Cornbread

## Ingredients:

- cooking spray
- ½ C. white cornmeal
- ½ C. flour
- 2 tsp. baking powder
- ½ tsp. salt
- 4 tsp. sugar
- 1 egg
- 2 tbsp. oil
- ½ C. milk

**Servings: 6**
**Cooking Time: 17 Mins.**

## Directions:

1. Preheat air fryer to 360°F.
2. Spray air fryer baking pan with nonstick cooking spray.
3. In a medium bowl, stir together the cornmeal, flour, baking powder, salt, and sugar.
4. In a small bowl, beat together the egg, oil, and milk. Stir into dry ingredients until well combined.
5. Pour batter into prepared baking pan.
6. Cook at 360°F for 17 minutes or until toothpick inserted in center comes out clean or with crumbs clinging.

# Roasted Tomato And Cheddar Rolls

## Ingredients:

- 4 Roma tomatoes
- ½ clove garlic, minced
- 1 tbsp. olive oil
- ¼ tsp. dried thyme
- salt and freshly ground black pepper
- 4 C. all-purpose flour
- 1 tsp. active dry yeast
- 2 tsp. sugar
- 2 tsp. salt
- 1 tbsp. olive oil
- 1 C. grated Cheddar cheese, plus more for sprinkling at the end
- 1½ C. water

## Directions:

1. Cut the Roma tomatoes in half, remove the seeds with your fingers and transfer to a bowl. Add the garlic, olive oil, dried thyme, salt and freshly ground black pepper and toss well.
2. Preheat the air fryer to 390°F.
3. Place the tomatoes, cut side up in the air fryer basket and air-fry for 10 minutes. The tomatoes should just start to brown. Shake the basket to redistribute the tomatoes, and air-fry for another 5 to 10 minutes at 330°F until the tomatoes are no longer juicy. Let the tomatoes cool and then rough chop them.
4. Combine the flour, yeast, sugar and salt in the bowl of a stand mixer. Add the olive oil, chopped roasted tomatoes and Cheddar cheese to the flour mixture and start to mix using the dough hook attachment. As you're mixing, add 1¼ C. of the water, mixing until the dough comes together. Continue to knead the dough with the dough hook for another 10 minutes, adding enough water to the dough to get it to the right consistency.
5. Transfer the dough to an oiled bowl, cover with a clean kitchen towel and let it rest and rise until it has doubled in volume – about 1 to 2 hours. Then, divide the dough into 12 equal portions. Roll each portion of dough into a ball. Lightly coat each dough ball with oil and let the dough balls rest and rise a second time, covered lightly with plastic wrap for 45 minutes. (Alternately, you can place the rolls in the refrigerator overnight and take them out 2 hours before you bake them.)
6. Preheat the air fryer to 360°F.
7. Spray the dough balls and the air fryer basket with a little olive oil. Place three rolls at a time in the basket and bake for 10 minutes. Add a little grated Cheddar cheese on top of the rolls for the last 2 minutes of air frying for an attractive finish.

# Chocolate Almond Crescent Rolls

## Ingredients:

- 1 (8-oz.) tube of crescent roll dough
- ⅔ C. semi-sweet or bittersweet chocolate chunks
- 1 egg white, lightly beaten
- ¼ C. sliced almonds
- powdered sugar, for dusting
- butter or oil

*Servings: 4*
*Cooking Time:*
*8 Mins.*

## Directions:

1. Preheat the air fryer to 350°F.

2. Unwrap the crescent roll dough and separate it into triangles with the points facing away from you. Place a row of chocolate chunks along the bottom edge of the dough. (If you are using chips, make it a double row.) Roll the dough up around the chocolate and then place another row of chunks on the dough. Roll again and finish with one or two chocolate chunks. Be sure to leave the end free of chocolate so that it can adhere to the rest of the roll.

3. Brush the tops of the crescent rolls with the lightly beaten egg white and sprinkle the almonds on top, pressing them into the crescent dough so they adhere.

4. Brush the bottom of the air fryer basket with butter or oil and transfer the crescent rolls to the basket. Air-fry at 350°F for 8 minutes. Remove and let the crescent rolls cool before dusting with powdered sugar and serving.

# Western Frittata

## Ingredients:

- ½ red or green bell pepper, cut into ½-inch chunks
- 1 tsp. olive oil
- 3 eggs, beaten
- ¼ C. grated Cheddar cheese
- ¼ C. diced cooked ham
- salt and freshly ground black pepper, to taste
- 1 tsp. butter
- 1 tsp. chopped fresh parsley

*Servings: 1*
*Cooking Time: 19 Mins.*

## Directions:

1. Preheat the air fryer to 400°F.
2. Toss the peppers with the olive oil and air-fry for 6 minutes, shaking the basket once or twice during the cooking process to redistribute the ingredients.
3. While the vegetables are cooking, beat the eggs well in a bowl, stir in the Cheddar cheese and ham, and season with salt and freshly ground black pepper. Add the air-fried peppers to this bowl when they have finished cooking.
4. Place a 6- or 7-inch non-stick metal cake pan into the air fryer basket with the butter using an aluminum sling to lower the pan into the basket. (Fold a piece of aluminum foil into a strip about 2-inches wide by 24-inches long.) Air-fry for 1 minute at 380°F to melt the butter. Remove the cake pan and rotate the pan to distribute the butter and grease the pan. Pour the egg mixture into the cake pan and return the pan to the air fryer, using the aluminum sling.
5. Air-fry at 380°F for 12 minutes, or until the frittata has puffed up and is lightly browned. Let the frittata sit in the air fryer for 5 minutes to cool to an edible temperature and set up. Remove the cake pan from the air fryer, sprinkle with parsley and serve immediately.

# Baked Eggs With Bacon-tomato Sauce

## Ingredients:

**Servings: 1**
**Cooking Time:**
**12 Mins.**

- 1 tsp. olive oil
- 2 tbsp. finely chopped onion
- 1 tsp. chopped fresh oregano
- pinch crushed red pepper flakes
- 1 (14-oz.) can crushed or diced tomatoes
- salt and freshly ground black pepper
- 2 slices of bacon, chopped
- 2 large eggs
- ¼ C. grated Cheddar cheese
- fresh parsley, chopped

## Directions:

1. Start by making the tomato sauce. Preheat a medium saucepan over medium heat on the stovetop. Add the olive oil and sauté the onion, oregano and pepper flakes for 5 minutes. Add the tomatoes and bring to a simmer. Season with salt and freshly ground black pepper and simmer for 10 minutes.

2. Meanwhile, Preheat the air fryer to 400°F and pour a little water into the bottom of the air fryer drawer. (This will help prevent the grease that drips into the bottom drawer from burning and smoking.) Place the bacon in the air fryer basket and air-fry at 400°F for 5 minutes, shaking the basket every once in a while.

3. When the bacon is almost crispy, remove it to a paper-towel lined plate and rinse out the air fryer drawer, draining away the bacon grease.

4. Transfer the tomato sauce to a shallow 7-inch pie dish. Crack the eggs on top of the sauce and scatter the cooked bacon back on top. Season with salt and freshly ground black pepper and transfer the pie dish into the air fryer basket. You can use an aluminum foil sling to help with this by taking a long piece of aluminum foil, folding it in half lengthwise twice until it is roughly 26-inches by 3-inches. Place this under the pie dish and hold the ends of the foil to move the pie dish in and out of the air fryer basket. Tuck the ends of the foil beside the pie dish while it cooks in the air fryer.

5. Air-fry at 400°F for 5 minutes, or until the eggs are almost cooked to your liking. Sprinkle cheese on top and air-fry for an additional 2 minutes. When the cheese has melted, remove the pie dish from the air fryer, sprinkle with a little chopped parsley and let the eggs cool for a few minutes – just enough time to toast some buttered bread in your air fryer!

# DESSERTS AND SWEETS

# Oreo-coated Peanut Butter Cups

## Ingredients:

- 8 Standard ¾-oz. peanut butter cups, frozen
- ⅓ C. All-purpose flour
- 2 Large egg white(s), beaten until foamy
- 16 Oreos or other creme-filled chocolate sandwich cookies, ground to crumbs in a food processor
- Vegetable oil spray

## Directions:

1. Set up and fill three shallow soup plates or small pie plates on your counter: one for the flour, one for the beaten egg white(s), and one for the cookie crumbs.

2. Dip a frozen peanut butter C. in the flour, turning it to coat all sides. Shake off any excess, then set it in the beaten egg white(s). Turn it to coat all sides, then let any excess egg white slip back into the rest. Set the candy bar in the cookie crumbs. Turn to coat on all parts, even the sides. Dip the peanut butter C. back in the egg white(s) as before, then into the cookie crumbs as before, making sure you have a solid, even coating all around the cup. Set aside while you dip and coat the remaining cups.

3. When all the peanut butter C. are dipped and coated, lightly coat them on all sides with the vegetable oil spray. Set them on a plate and freeze while the air fryer heats.

4. Preheat the air fryer to 400°F.

5. Set the dipped C. wider side up in the basket with as much air space between them as possible. Air-fry undisturbed for 4 minutes, or until they feel soft but the coating is set.

6. Turn off the machine and remove the basket from it. Set aside the basket with the fried C. for 10 minutes. Use a nonstick-safe spatula to transfer the fried C. to a wire rack. Cool for at least another 5 minutes before serving.

# Cinnamon Sugar Banana Rolls

## Ingredients:

- ¼ C. Granulated white sugar
- 2 tsp. Ground cinnamon
- 2 tbsp. Peach or apricot jam or orange marmalade
- 6 Spring roll wrappers, thawed if necessary
- 2 Ripe banana(s), peeled and cut into 3-inch-long sections
- 1 Large egg, well beaten
- Vegetable oil spray

*Servings: 6*
*Cooking Time: 8 Mins.*

## Directions:

1. Preheat the air fryer to 400°F.
2. Stir the sugar and cinnamon in a small bowl until well combined. Stir the jam or marmalade with a fork to loosen it up.
3. Set a spring roll wrapper on a clean, dry work surface. Roll a banana section in the sugar mixture until evenly and well coated. Set the coated banana along one edge of the wrapper. Top it with about 1 tsp. of the jam or marmalade. Fold the sides of the wrapper perpendicular to the banana up and over the banana, partially covering it. Brush beaten egg over the side of the wrapper farthest from the banana. Starting with the banana, roll the wrapper closed, ending at the part with the beaten egg. Press gently to seal. Set the roll aside seam side down and continue filling and rolling the remaining wrappers in the same way.
4. Lightly coat the wrappers with vegetable oil spray. Set them seam side down in the basket with as much air space between them as possible. Air-fry undisturbed for 8 minutes, or until crisp and golden brown.
5. Use kitchen tongs to gently transfer the rolls to a wire rack. Cool for at least 5 minutes or up to 30 minutes before serving.

# Mixed Berry Hand Pies

## Ingredients:

- ¾ C. sugar
- ½ tsp. ground cinnamon
- 1 tbsp. cornstarch
- 1 C. blueberries
- 1 C. blackberries
- 1 C. raspberries, divided
- 1 tsp. water
- 1 package refrigerated pie dough (or your own homemade pie dough)
- 1 egg, beaten

*Servings: 4*
*Cooking Time: 15 Mins.*

## Directions:

1. Combine the sugar, cinnamon, and cornstarch in a small saucepan. Add the blueberries, blackberries, and ½ C. of the raspberries. Toss the berries gently to coat them evenly. Add the tsp. of water to the saucepan and turn the stovetop on to medium-high heat, stirring occasionally. Once the berries break down, release their juice and start to simmer (about 5 minutes), simmer for another couple of minutes and then transfer the mixture to a bowl, stir in the remaining ½ C. of raspberries and let it cool.

2. Preheat the air fryer to 370°F.

3. Cut the pie dough into four 5-inch circles and four 6-inch circles.

4. Spread the 6-inch circles on a flat surface. Divide the berry filling between all four circles. Brush the perimeter of the dough circles with a little water. Place the 5-inch circles on top of the filling and press the perimeter of the dough circles together to seal. Roll the edges of the bottom circle up over the top circle to make a crust around the filling. Press a fork around the crust to make decorative indentations and to seal the crust shut. Brush the pies with egg wash and sprinkle a little sugar on top. Poke a small hole in the center of each pie with a paring knife to vent the dough.

5. Air-fry two pies at a time. Brush or spray the air fryer basket with oil and place the pies into the basket. Air-fry for 9 minutes. Turn the pies over and air-fry for another 6 minutes. Serve warm or at room temperature.

# White Chocolate Cranberry Blondies

## Ingredients:

**Servings: 6
Cooking Time:
18 Mins.**

- ⅓ C. butter
- ½ C. sugar
- 1 tsp. vanilla extract
- 1 large egg
- 1 C. all-purpose flour
- ½ tsp. baking powder
- ⅛ tsp. salt
- ¼ C. dried cranberries
- ¼ C. white chocolate chips

## Directions:

1. Preheat the air fryer to 320°F.
2. In a large bowl, cream the butter with the sugar and vanilla extract. Whisk in the egg and set aside.
3. In a separate bowl, mix the flour with the baking powder and salt. Then gently mix the dry ingredients into the wet. Fold in the cranberries and chocolate chips.
4. Liberally spray an oven-safe 7-inch springform pan with olive oil and pour the batter into the pan.
5. Cook for 17 minutes or until a toothpick inserted in the center comes out clean.
6. Remove and let cool 5 minutes before serving.

# Sugared Pizza Dough Dippers With Raspberry Cream Cheese Dip

## Ingredients:

- 1 lb. pizza dough*
- ½ C. butter, melted
- ¾ to 1 C. sugar
- Raspberry Cream Cheese Dip
- 4 oz. cream cheese, softened
- 2 tbsp. powdered sugar
- ½ tsp. almond extract or almond paste
- 1½ tbsp. milk
- ¼ C. raspberry preserves
- fresh raspberries

**Servings: 10**
**Cooking Time: 8 Mins.**

## Directions:

1. Cut the ingredients in half or save half of the dough for another recipe.
2. When you're ready to make your sugared dough dippers, remove your pizza dough from the refrigerator at least 1 hour prior to baking and let it sit on the counter, covered gently with plastic wrap.
3. Roll the dough into two 15-inch logs. Cut each log into 20 slices and roll each slice so that it is 3- to 3½-inches long. Cut each slice in half and twist the dough halves together 3 to 4 times. Place the twisted dough on a cookie sheet, brush with melted butter and sprinkle sugar over the dough twists.
4. Preheat the air fryer to 350°F.
5. Brush the bottom of the air fryer basket with a little melted butter. Air-fry the dough twists in batches. Place 8 to 12 (depending on the size of your air fryer) in the air fryer basket.
6. Air-fry for 6 minutes. Turn the dough strips over and brush the other side with butter. Air-fry for an additional 2 minutes.
7. While the dough twists are cooking, make the cream cheese and raspberry dip. Whip the cream cheese with a hand mixer until fluffy. Add the powdered sugar, almond extract and milk, and beat until smooth. Fold in the raspberry preserves and transfer to a serving dish.
8. As the batches of dough twists are complete, place them into a shallow dish. Brush with more melted butter and generously coat with sugar, shaking the dish to cover both sides. Serve the sugared dough dippers warm with the raspberry cream cheese dip on the side. Garnish with fresh raspberries.

# Maple Cinnamon Cheesecake

## Ingredients:

- 6 sheets of cinnamon graham crackers
- 2 tbsp. butter
- 8 oz. Neufchâtel cream cheese
- 3 tbsp. pure maple syrup
- 1 large egg
- ½ tsp. ground cinnamon
- ¼ tsp. salt

**Servings: 4**
**Cooking Time:**
**12 Mins.**

## Directions:

1. Preheat the air fryer to 350°F.
2. Place the graham crackers in a food processor and process until crushed into a flour. Mix with the butter and press into a mini air-fryer-safe pan lined at the bottom with parchment paper. Place in the air fryer and cook for 4 minutes.
3. In a large bowl, place the cream cheese and maple syrup. Use a hand mixer or stand mixer and beat together until smooth. Add in the egg, cinnamon, and salt and mix on medium speed until combined.
4. Remove the graham cracker crust from the air fryer and pour the batter into the pan.
5. Place the pan back in the air fryer, adjusting the temperature to 315°F. Cook for 18 minutes. Carefully remove when cooking completes. The top should be lightly browned and firm.
6. Keep the cheesecake in the pan and place in the refrigerator for 3 or more hours to firm up before serving.

# Sea-salted Caramel Cookie Cups

## Ingredients:

- ⅓ C. butter
- ¼ C. brown sugar
- 1 tsp. vanilla extract
- 1 large egg
- 1 C. all-purpose flour
- ½ C. old-fashioned oats
- ½ tsp. baking soda
- ¼ tsp. salt
- ⅓ C. sea-salted caramel chips

*Servings: 12*
*Cooking Time: 12 Mins.*

## Directions:

1. Preheat the air fryer to 300°F.
2. In a large bowl, cream the butter with the brown sugar and vanilla. Whisk in the egg and set aside.
3. In a separate bowl, mix the flour, oats, baking soda, and salt. Then gently mix the dry ingredients into the wet. Fold in the caramel chips.
4. Divide the batter into 12 silicon muffin liners. Place the cookie C. into the air fryer basket and cook for 12 minutes or until a toothpick inserted in the center comes out clean.
5. Remove and let cool 5 minutes before serving.

# Peanut Butter C. Doughnut Holes

## Ingredients:

- 1½ C. bread flour
- 1 tsp. active dry yeast
- 1 tbsp. sugar
- ¼ tsp. salt
- ½ C. warm milk
- ½ tsp. vanilla extract
- 2 egg yolks
- 2 tbsp. melted butter
- 24 miniature peanut butter cups, plus a few more for garnish
- vegetable oil, in a spray bottle
- Doughnut Topping
- 1 C. chocolate chips
- 2 tbsp. milk

## Directions:

1. Combine the flour, yeast, sugar and salt in a bowl. Add the milk, vanilla, egg yolks and butter. Mix well until the dough starts to come together. Transfer the dough to a floured surface and knead by hand for 2 minutes. Shape the dough into a ball and transfer it to a large oiled bowl. Cover the bowl with a towel and let the dough rise in a warm place for 1 to 1½ hours, until the dough has doubled in size.

2. When the dough has risen, punch it down and roll it into a 24-inch long log. Cut the dough into 24 pieces. Push a peanut butter C. into the center of each piece of dough, pinch the dough shut and roll it into a ball. Place the dough balls on a cookie sheet and let them rise in a warm place for 30 minutes.

3. Preheat the air fryer to 400°F.

4. Spray or brush the dough balls lightly with vegetable oil. Air-fry eight at a time, at 400°F for 4 minutes, turning them over halfway through the cooking process.

5. While the doughnuts are air frying, prepare the topping. Place the chocolate chips and milk in a microwave safe bowl. Microwave on high for 1 minute. Stir and microwave for an additional 30 seconds if necessary to get all the chips to melt. Stir until the chips are melted and smooth.

6. Dip the top half of the doughnut holes into the melted chocolate. Place them on a rack to set up for just a few minutes and watch them disappear.

# Chewy Coconut Cake

## Ingredients:

- ¾ C. plus 2½ tbsp. All-purpose flour
- ¾ tsp. Baking powder
- ⅛ tsp. Table salt
- 7½ tbsp. (1 stick minus ½ tablespoon) Butter, at room temperature
- ⅓ C. plus 1 tbsp. Granulated white sugar
- 5 tbsp. Packed light brown sugar
- 5 tbsp. Pasteurized egg substitute, such as Egg Beaters
- 2 tsp. Vanilla extract
- ½ C. Unsweetened shredded coconut (see here)
- Baking spray

**Servings: 6**
**Cooking Time: 18-22 Mins.**

## Directions:

1. Preheat the air fryer to 325°F (or 330°F, if that's the closest setting).
2. Mix the flour, baking powder, and salt in a small bowl until well combined.
3. Using an electric hand mixer at medium speed , beat the butter, granulated white sugar, and brown sugar in a medium bowl until creamy and smooth, about 3 minutes, occasionally scraping down the inside of the bowl. Beat in the egg substitute or egg and vanilla until smooth.
4. Scrape down and remove the beaters. Fold in the flour mixture with a rubber spatula just until all the flour is moistened. Fold in the coconut until the mixture is a uniform color.
5. Use the baking spray to generously coat the inside of a 6-inch round cake pan for a small batch, a 7-inch round cake pan for a medium batch, or an 8-inch round cake pan for a large batch. Scrape and spread the batter into the pan, smoothing the batter out to an even layer.
6. Set the pan in the basket and air-fry for 18 minutes for a 6-inch layer, 20 minutes for a 7-inch layer, or 22 minutes for an 8-inch layer, or until the cake is well browned and set even if there's a little soft give right at the center. Start checking it at the 16-minute mark to know where you are.
7. Use hot pads or silicone baking mitts to transfer the cake pan to a wire rack. Cool for at least 1 hour or up to 4 hours. Use a nonstick-safe knife to slice the cake into wedges right in the pan, lifting them out one by one.

# Coconut Macaroons

## Ingredients:

- 1⅓ C. shredded, sweetened coconut
- 4½ tsp. flour
- 2 tbsp. sugar
- 1 egg white
- ½ tsp. almond extract

## Directions:

1. Preheat air fryer to 330°F.
2. Mix all ingredients together.
3. Shape coconut mixture into 12 balls.
4. Place all 12 macaroons in air fryer basket. They won't expand, so you can place them close together, but they shouldn't touch.
5. Cook at 330°F for 8 minutes, until golden.

# Gingerbread

## Ingredients:

- cooking spray
- 1 C. flour
- 2 tbsp. sugar
- ¾ tsp. ground ginger
- ¼ tsp. cinnamon
- 1 tsp. baking powder
- ½ tsp. baking soda
- ⅛ tsp. salt
- 1 egg
- ¼ C. molasses
- ½ C. buttermilk
- 2 tbsp. oil
- 1 tsp. pure vanilla extract

## Directions:

1. Preheat air fryer to 330°F.
2. Spray 6 x 6-inch baking dish lightly with cooking spray.
3. In a medium bowl, mix together all the dry ingredients.
4. In a separate bowl, beat the egg. Add molasses, buttermilk, oil, and vanilla and stir until well mixed.
5. Pour liquid mixture into dry ingredients and stir until well blended.
6. Pour batter into baking dish and cook at 330°F for 20minutes or until toothpick inserted in center of loaf comes out clean.

# FISH AND SEAFOOD RECIPES

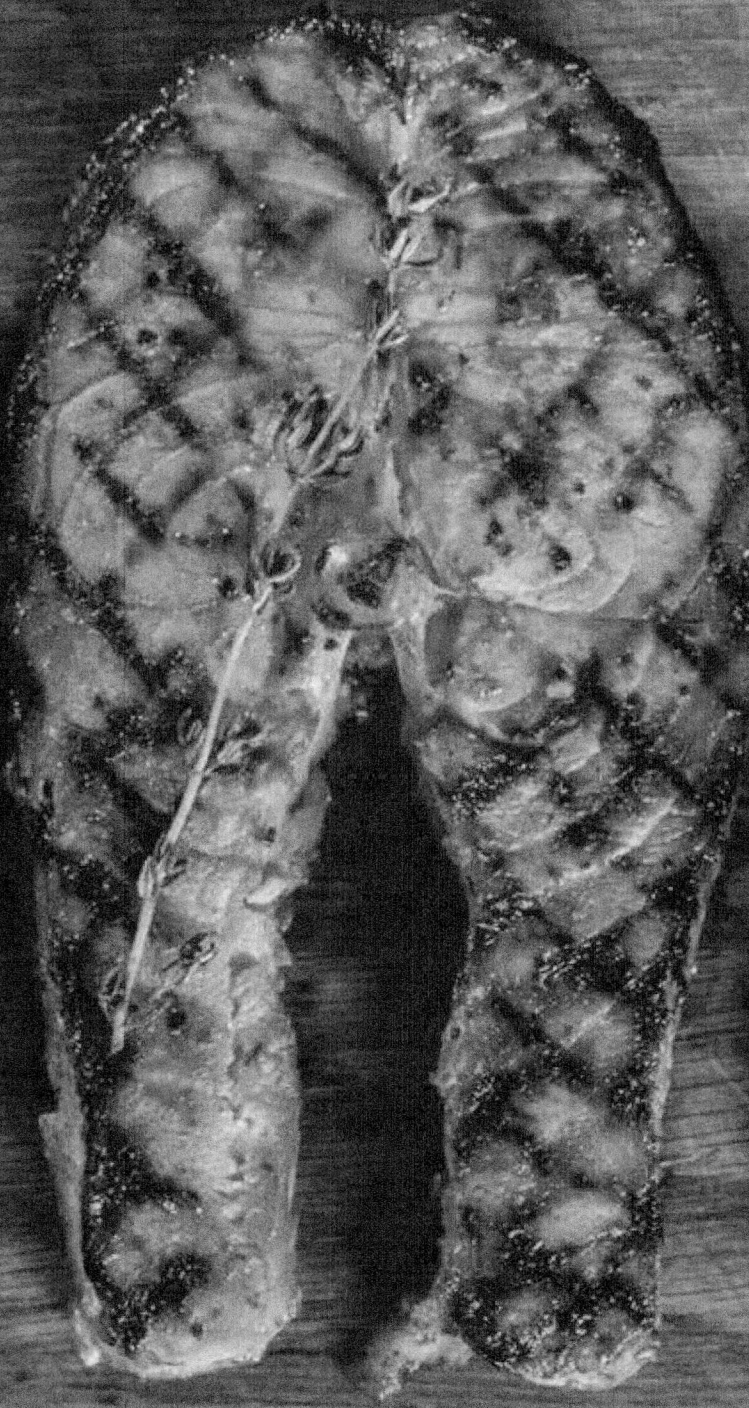

# Maple Balsamic Glazed Salmon

## Ingredients:

- 4 (6-oz.) fillets of salmon
- salt and freshly ground black pepper
- vegetable oil
- ¼ C. pure maple syrup
- 3 tbsp. balsamic vinegar
- 1 tsp. Dijon mustard

*Servings: 4*
*Cooking Time:*
*10 Mins.*

## Directions:

1. Preheat the air fryer to 400°F.
2. Season the salmon well with salt and freshly ground black pepper. Spray or brush the bottom of the air fryer basket with vegetable oil and place the salmon fillets inside. Air-fry the salmon for 5 minutes.
3. While the salmon is air-frying, combine the maple syrup, balsamic vinegar and Dijon mustard in a small saucepan over medium heat and stir to blend well. Let the mixture simmer while the fish is cooking. It should start to thicken slightly, but keep your eye on it so it doesn't burn.
4. Brush the glaze on the salmon fillets and air-fry for an additional 5 minutes. The salmon should feel firm to the touch when finished and the glaze should be nicely browned on top. Brush a little more glaze on top before removing and serving with rice and vegetables, or a nice green salad.

# Fish Sticks With Tartar Sauce

## Ingredients:

- 12 oz. cod or flounder
- ½ C. flour
- ½ tsp. paprika
- 1 tsp. salt
- lots of freshly ground black pepper
- 2 eggs, lightly beaten
- 1½ C. panko breadcrumbs
- 1 tsp. salt
- vegetable oil
- Tartar Sauce:
- ¼ C. mayonnaise
- 2 tsp. lemon juice
- 2 tbsp. finely chopped sweet pickles
- salt and freshly ground black pepper

*Servings: 2*
*Cooking Time:*
*6 Mins.*

## Directions:

1. Cut the fish into ¾-inch wide sticks or strips. Set up a dredging station. Combine the flour, paprika, salt and pepper in a shallow dish. Beat the eggs lightly in a second shallow dish. Finally, mix the breadcrumbs and salt in a third shallow dish. Coat the fish sticks by dipping the fish into the flour, then the egg and finally the breadcrumbs, coating on all sides in each step and pressing the crumbs firmly onto the fish. Place the finished sticks on a plate or baking sheet while you finish all the sticks.
2. Preheat the air fryer to 400°F.
3. Spray the fish sticks with the oil and spray or brush the bottom of the air fryer basket. Place the fish into the basket and air-fry at 400°F for 4 minutes, turn the fish sticks over, and air-fry for another 2 minutes.
4. While the fish is cooking, mix the tartar sauce ingredients together.
5. Serve the fish sticks warm with the tartar sauce and some French fries on the side.

# Shrimp

## Ingredients:

- 1 lb. (26–30 count) shrimp, peeled, deveined, and butterflied (last tail section of shell intact)
- Marinade
- 1 5-oz. can evaporated milk
- 2 eggs, beaten
- 2 tbsp. white vinegar
- 1 tbsp. baking powder
- Coating
- 1 C. crushed panko breadcrumbs
- ½ tsp. paprika
- ½ tsp. Old Bay Seasoning
- ¼ tsp. garlic powder
- oil for misting or cooking spray

*Servings: 4*
*Cooking Time: 8 Mins.*

## Directions:

1. Stir together all marinade ingredients until well mixed. Add shrimp and stir to coat. Refrigerate for 1 hour.
2. When ready to cook, preheat air fryer to 390°F.
3. Combine coating ingredients in shallow dish.
4. Remove shrimp from marinade, roll in crumb mixture, and spray with olive oil or cooking spray.
5. Cooking in two batches, place shrimp in air fryer basket in single layer, close but not overlapping. Cook at 390°F for 8 minutes, until light golden brown and crispy.
6. Repeat step 5 to cook remaining shrimp.

# Bacon-wrapped Scallops

## Ingredients:

- 16 large scallops
- 8 bacon strips
- ½ tsp. black pepper
- ¼ tsp. smoked paprika

*Servings: 4*
*Cooking Time:*
*8 Mins.*

## Directions:

1. Pat the scallops dry with a paper towel. Slice each of the bacon strips in half. Wrap 1 bacon strip around 1 scallop and secure with a toothpick. Repeat with the remaining scallops. Season the scallops with pepper and paprika.
2. Preheat the air fryer to 350°F.
3. Place the bacon-wrapped scallops in the air fryer basket and cook for 4 minutes, shake the basket, cook another 3 minutes, shake the basket, and cook another 1 to 3 to minutes. When the bacon is crispy, the scallops should be cooked through and slightly firm, but not rubbery. Serve immediately.

# Blackened Red Snapper

## Ingredients:

- 1½ tsp. black pepper
- ¼ tsp. thyme
- ¼ tsp. garlic powder
- ⅛ tsp. cayenne pepper
- 1 tsp. olive oil
- 4 4-oz. red snapper fillet portions, skin on
- 4 thin slices lemon
- cooking spray

*Servings: 4*
*Cooking Time:*
*8 Mins.*

## Directions:

1. Mix the spices and oil together to make a paste. Rub into both sides of the fish.
2. Spray air fryer basket with nonstick cooking spray and lay snapper steaks in basket, skin-side down.
3. Place a lemon slice on each piece of fish.
4. Cook at 390°F for 8 minutes. The fish will not flake when done, but it should be white through the center.

# Fish-in-chips

## Ingredients:

- 1 C. All-purpose flour or potato starch
- 2 Large egg(s), well beaten
- 1½ C. (6 ounces) Crushed plain potato chips, preferably thick-cut or ruffled (gluten-free, if a concern)
- 4 4-oz. skinless cod fillets

***Servings: 4***
***Cooking Time:***
***11 Mins.***

## Directions:

1. Preheat the air fryer to 400°F.
2. Set up and fill three shallow soup plates or small pie plates on your counter: one for the flour, one for the beaten egg(s), and one for the crushed potato chips.
3. Dip a piece of cod in the flour, turning it to coat on all sides, even the ends and sides. Gently shake off any excess flour, then dip it in the beaten egg(s). Gently turn to coat it on all sides, then let any excess egg slip back into the rest. Set the fillet in the crushed potato chips and turn several times and onto all sides, pressing gently to coat the fish. Dip it back in the egg(s), coating all sides but taking care that the coating doesn't slip off; then dip it back in the potato chips for a thick, even coating. Set it aside and coat more fillets in the same way.
4. When the machine is at temperature, set the fillets in the basket with as much air space between them as possible. Air-fry undisturbed for 11 minutes, until golden brown and firm but not hard.
5. Use kitchen tongs to transfer the fillets to a wire rack. Cool for just a minute or two before serving.

# Sweet Potato–wrapped Shrimp

## Ingredients:

- 24 Long spiralized sweet potato strands
- Olive oil spray
- ¼ tsp. Garlic powder
- ¼ tsp. Table salt
- Up to a ⅛ tsp. Cayenne
- 12 Large shrimp (20–25 per pound), peeled and deveined

*Servings: 3*
*Cooking Time: 6 Mins.*

## Directions:

1. Preheat the air fryer to 400°F.
2. Lay the spiralized sweet potato strands on a large swath of paper towels and straighten out the strands to long ropes. Coat them with olive oil spray, then sprinkle them with the garlic powder, salt, and cayenne.
3. Pick up 2 strands and wrap them around the center of a shrimp, with the ends tucked under what now becomes the bottom side of the shrimp. Continue wrapping the remainder of the shrimp.
4. Set the shrimp bottom side down in the basket with as much air space between them as possible. Air-fry undisturbed for 6 minutes, or until the sweet potato strands are crisp and the shrimp are pink and firm.
5. Use kitchen tongs to transfer the shrimp to a wire rack. Cool for only a minute or two before serving.

# BEEF, PORK & LAMB RECIPES

# Meatloaf With Tangy Tomato Glaze

## Ingredients:

*Servings: 6*
*Cooking Time: 50 Mins.*

- 1 lb. ground beef
- ½ lb. ground pork
- ½ lb. ground veal (or turkey)
- 1 medium onion, diced
- 1 small clove of garlic, minced
- 2 egg yolks, lightly beaten
- ½ C. tomato ketchup
- 1 tbsp. Worcestershire sauce
- ½ C. plain breadcrumbs*
- 2 tsp. salt
- freshly ground black pepper
- ½ C. chopped fresh parsley, plus more for garnish
- 6 tbsp. ketchup
- 1 tbsp. balsamic vinegar
- 2 tbsp. brown sugar

## Directions:

1. Combine the meats, onion, garlic, egg yolks, ketchup, Worcestershire sauce, breadcrumbs, salt, pepper and fresh parsley in a large bowl and mix well.
2. Preheat the air fryer to 350°F and pour a little water into the bottom of the air fryer drawer. (This will help prevent the grease that drips into the bottom drawer from burning and smoking.)
3. Transfer the meatloaf mixture to the air fryer basket, packing it down gently. Run a spatula around the meatloaf to create a space about ½-inch wide between the meat and the side of the air fryer basket.
4. Air-fry at 350°F for 20 minutes. Carefully invert the meatloaf onto a plate (remember to remove the basket from the air fryer drawer so you don't pour all the grease out) and slide it back into the air fryer basket to turn it over. Re-shape the meatloaf with a spatula if necessary. Air-fry for another 20 minutes at 350°F.
5. Combine the ketchup, balsamic vinegar and brown sugar in a bowl and spread the mixture over the meatloaf. Air-fry for another 10 minutes, until an instant read thermometer inserted into the center of the meatloaf registers 160°F.
6. Allow the meatloaf to rest for a few more minutes and then transfer it to a serving platter using a spatula. Slice the meatloaf, sprinkle a little chopped parsley on top if desired, and serve.

# Barbecue Country-style Pork Ribs

## Ingredients:

- 3 8-oz. boneless country-style pork ribs
- 1½ tsp. Mild smoked paprika
- 1½ tsp. Light brown sugar
- ¾ tsp. Onion powder
- ¾ tsp. Ground black pepper
- ¼ tsp. Table salt
- Vegetable oil spray

*Servings: 3*
*Cooking Time: 30 Mins.*

## Directions:

1. Preheat the air fryer to 350°F. Set the ribs in a bowl on the counter as the machine heats.
2. Mix the smoked paprika, brown sugar, onion powder, pepper, and salt in a small bowl until well combined. Rub this mixture over all the surfaces of the country-style ribs. Generously coat the country-style ribs with vegetable oil spray.
3. Set the ribs in the basket with as much air space between them as possible. Air-fry undisturbed for 30 minutes, or until browned and sizzling and an instant-read meat thermometer inserted into one rib registers at least 145°F.
4. Use kitchen tongs to transfer the country-style ribs to a wire rack. Cool for 5 minutes before serving.

# Lemon-butter Veal Cutlets

## Ingredients:

- 3 strips Butter (see step 2)
- 3 Thinly pounded 2-oz. veal leg cutlets (less than ¼ inch thick)
- ¼ tsp. Lemon-pepper seasoning

**Servings: 2**
**Cooking Time:**
**4 Mins.**

## Directions:

1. Preheat the air fryer to 400°F.

2. Run a vegetable peeler lengthwise along a hard, cold stick of butter, making 2, 3, or 4 long strips as the recipe requires for the number of cutlets you're making.

3. Lay the veal cutlets on a clean, dry cutting board or work surface. Sprinkle about ⅛ tsp. lemon-pepper seasoning over each. Set a strip of butter on top of each cutlet.

4. When the machine is at temperature, set the topped cutlets in the basket so that they don't overlap or even touch. Air-fry undisturbed for 4 minutes without turning.

5. Use a nonstick-safe spatula to transfer the cutlets to a serving plate or plates, taking care to keep as much of the butter on top as possible. Remove the basket from the drawer or from over the baking tray. Carefully pour the browned butter over the cutlets.

# Sausage-cheese Calzone

## Ingredients:

**Servings: 8**
**Cooking Time: 8 Mins.**

- Crust
- 2 C. white wheat flour, plus more for kneading and rolling
- 1 package (¼ ounce) RapidRise yeast
- 1 tsp. salt
- ½ tsp. dried basil
- 1 C. warm water (115°F to 125°F)
- 2 tsp. olive oil
- Filling
- ¼ lb. Italian sausage
- ½ C. ricotta cheese
- 4 oz. mozzarella cheese, shredded
- ¼ C. grated Parmesan cheese
- oil for misting or cooking spray
- marinara sauce for serving

## Directions:

1. Crumble Italian sausage into air fryer baking pan and cook at 390°F for 5minutes. Stir, breaking apart, and cook for 3 to 4minutes, until well done. Remove and set aside on paper towels to drain.
2. To make dough, combine flour, yeast, salt, and basil. Add warm water and oil and stir until a soft dough forms. Turn out onto lightly floured board and knead for 3 or 4minutes. Let dough rest for 10minutes.
3. To make filling, combine the three cheeses in a medium bowl and mix well. Stir in the cooked sausage.
4. Cut dough into 8 pieces.
5. Working with 4 pieces of the dough, press each into a circle about 5 inches in diameter. Top each dough circle with 2 heaping tbsp. of filling. Fold over to create a half-moon shape and press edges firmly together. Be sure that edges are firmly sealed to prevent leakage. Spray both sides with oil or cooking spray.
6. Place 4 calzones in air fryer basket and cook at 360°F for 5minutes. Mist with oil and cook for 3 minutes, until crust is done and nicely browned.
7. While the first batch is cooking, press out the remaining dough, fill, and shape into calzones.
8. Spray both sides with oil and cook for 5minutes. If needed, mist with oil and continue cooking for 3 minutes longer. This second batch will cook a little faster than the first because your air fryer is already hot.
9. Serve with marinara sauce on the side for dipping.

# Steakhouse Burgers With Red Onion Compote

## Ingredients:

- 1½ lb. lean ground beef
- 2 cloves garlic, minced and divided
- 1 tsp. Worcestershire sauce
- 1 tsp. sea salt, divided
- ½ tsp. black pepper
- 1 tbsp. extra-virgin olive oil
- 1 red onion, thinly sliced
- ¼ C. balsamic vinegar
- 1 tsp. sugar
- 1 tbsp. tomato paste
- 2 tbsp. mayonnaise
- 2 tbsp. sour cream
- 4 brioche hamburger buns
- 1 C. arugula

*Servings: 4*
*Cooking Time: 22 Mins.*

## Directions:

1. In a large bowl, mix together the ground beef, 1 of the minced garlic cloves, the Worcestershire sauce, ½ tsp. of the salt, and the black pepper. Form the meat into 1-inch-thick patties. Make a dent in the center (this helps the center cook evenly). Let the meat sit for 15 minutes.

2. Meanwhile, in a small saucepan over medium heat, cook the olive oil and red onion for 4 minutes, stirring frequently to avoid burning. Add in the balsamic vinegar, sugar, and tomato paste, and cook for an additional 3 minutes, stirring frequently. Transfer the onion compote to a small bowl.

3. Preheat the air fryer to 350°F.

4. In another small bowl, mix together the remaining minced garlic, the mayonnaise, and the sour cream. Spread the mayo mixture on the insides of the brioche buns.

5. Cook the hamburgers for 6 minutes, flip the burgers, and cook an additional 2 to 6 minutes. Check the internal temperature to avoid under- or overcooking. Hamburgers should be cooked to at least 160°F. After cooking, cover with foil and let the meat rest for 5 minutes.

6. Meanwhile, place the buns inside the air fryer and toast them for 3 minutes.

7. To assemble the burgers, place the hamburger on one side of the bun, top with onion compote and ¼ C. arugula, and then place the other half of the bun on top.

# Lamb Meatballs With Quick Tomato Sauce

## Ingredients:

*Servings: 4*
*Cooking Time:*
*8 Mins.*

- ½ small onion, finely diced
- 1 clove garlic, minced
- 1 lb. ground lamb
- 2 tbsp. fresh parsley, finely chopped (plus more for garnish)
- 2 tsp. fresh oregano, finely chopped
- 2 tbsp. milk
- 1 egg yolk
- salt and freshly ground black pepper
- ½ C. crumbled feta cheese, for garnish
- Tomato Sauce:
- 2 tbsp. butter
- 1 clove garlic, smashed
- pinch crushed red pepper flakes
- ¼ tsp. ground cinnamon
- 1 (28-oz.) can crushed tomatoes
- salt, to taste

## Directions:

1. Combine all ingredients for the meatballs in a large bowl and mix just until everything is combined. Shape the mixture into 1½-inch balls or shape the meat between two spoons to make quenelles (little three-sided footballs).
2. Preheat the air fryer to 400°F.
3. While the air fryer is Preheating, start the quick tomato sauce. Place the butter, garlic and red pepper flakes in a sauté pan and heat over medium heat on the stovetop. Let the garlic sizzle a little, but before the butter starts to brown, add the cinnamon and tomatoes. Bring to a simmer and simmer for 15 minutes. Season to taste with salt (but not too much as the feta that you will be sprinkling on at the end will be salty).
4. Brush the bottom of the air fryer basket with a little oil and transfer the meatballs to the air fryer basket in one layer, air-frying in batches if necessary.
5. Air-fry at 400°F for 8 minutes, giving the basket a shake once during the cooking process to turn the meatballs over.
6. To serve, spoon a pool of the tomato sauce onto plates and add the meatballs in a decorative manner. Sprinkle the feta cheese on top and garnish with more fresh parsley. Serve immediately.

# Vietnamese Shaking Beef

## Ingredients:

- 1 lb. Beef tenderloin, cut into 1-inch cubes
- 1 tbsp. Regular or low-sodium soy sauce or gluten-free tamari sauce
- 1 tbsp. Fish sauce (gluten-free, if a concern)
- 1 tbsp. Dark brown sugar
- 1½ tsp. Ground black pepper
- 3 Medium scallions, trimmed and thinly sliced
- 2 tbsp. Butter
- 1½ tsp. Minced garlic

*Servings: 3*
*Cooking Time:*
*7 Mins.*

## Directions:

1. Mix the beef, soy or tamari sauce, fish sauce, and brown sugar in a bowl until well combined. Cover and refrigerate for at least 2 hours or up to 8 hours, tossing the beef at least twice in the marinade.

2. Put a 6-inch round or square cake pan in an air-fryer basket for a small batch, a 7-inch round or square cake pan for a medium batch, or an 8-inch round or square cake pan for a large one. Or put one of these on the rack of a toaster oven–style air fryer. Heat the machine with the pan in it to 400°F. When the machine it at temperature, let the pan sit in the heat for 2 to 3 minutes so that it gets very hot.

3. Use a slotted spoon to transfer the beef to the pan, leaving any marinade behind in the bowl. Spread the meat into as close to an even layer as you can. Air-fry undisturbed for 5 minutes. Meanwhile, discard the marinade, if any.

4. Add the scallions, butter, and garlic to the beef. Air-fry for 2 minutes, tossing and rearranging the beef and scallions repeatedly, perhaps every 20 seconds.

5. Remove the basket from the machine and let the meat cool in the pan for a couple of minutes before serving.

# Tuscan Veal Chops

## Ingredients:

- 4 tsp. Olive oil
- 2 tsp. Finely minced garlic
- 2 tsp. Finely minced fresh rosemary leaves
- 1 tsp. Finely grated lemon zest
- 1 tsp. Crushed fennel seeds
- 1 tsp. Table salt
- Up to ¼ tsp. Red pepper flakes
- 2 10-oz. bone-in veal loin or rib chop(s), about ½ inch thick

## Directions:

1. Preheat the air fryer to 400°F.
2. Mix the oil, garlic, rosemary, lemon zest, fennel seeds, salt, and red pepper flakes in a small bowl. Rub this mixture onto both sides of the veal chop(s). Set aside at room temperature as the machine comes to temperature.
3. Set the chop(s) in the basket. If you're cooking more than one chop, leave as much air space between them as possible. Air-fry undisturbed for 12 minutes for medium-rare, or until an instant-read meat thermometer inserted into the center of a chop (without touching bone) registers 135°F (not USDA-approved). Or air-fry undisturbed for 15 minutes for medium-well, or until an instant-read meat thermometer registers 145°F (USDA-approved).
4. Use kitchen tongs to transfer the chops to a cutting board or a wire rack. Cool for 5 minutes before serving.

# POULTRY RECIPES

# Chicken Adobo

## Ingredients:

- 6 boneless chicken thighs
- ¼ C. soy sauce or tamari
- ½ C. rice wine vinegar
- 4 cloves garlic, minced
- ⅛ tsp. crushed red pepper flakes
- ½ tsp. black pepper

*Servings: 6*
*Cooking Time:*
*12 Mins.*

## Directions:

1. Place the chicken thighs into a resealable plastic bag with the soy sauce or tamari, the rice wine vinegar, the garlic, and the crushed red pepper flakes. Seal the bag and let the chicken marinate at least 1 hour in the refrigerator.
2. Preheat the air fryer to 400°F.
3. Drain the chicken and pat dry with a paper towel. Season the chicken with black pepper and liberally spray with cooking spray.
4. Place the chicken in the air fryer basket and cook for 9 minutes, turn over at 9 minutes and check for an internal temperature of 165°F, and cook another 3 minutes.

# Poblano Bake

## Ingredients:

- 2 large poblano peppers (approx. 5½ inches long excluding stem)
- ¾ lb. ground turkey, raw
- ¾ C. cooked brown rice
- 1 tsp. chile powder
- ½ tsp. ground cumin
- ½ tsp. garlic powder
- 4 oz. sharp Cheddar cheese, grated
- 1 8-oz. jar salsa, warmed

**Servings: 4**
**Cooking Time:**
**11 Minutes**

## Directions:

1. Slice each pepper in half lengthwise so that you have four wide, flat pepper halves.
2. Remove seeds and membrane and discard. Rinse inside and out.
3. In a large bowl, combine turkey, rice, chile powder, cumin, and garlic powder. Mix well.
4. Divide turkey filling into 4 portions and stuff one into each of the 4 pepper halves. Press lightly to pack down.
5. Place 2 pepper halves in air fryer basket and cook at 390°F for 10minutes or until turkey is well done.
6. Top each pepper half with ¼ of the grated cheese. Cook 1 more minute or just until cheese melts.
7. Repeat steps 5 and 6 to cook remaining pepper halves.
8. To serve, place each pepper half on a plate and top with ¼ C. warm salsa.

# Chicken Souvlaki Gyros

## Ingredients:

**Servings: 4**
**Cooking Time:**
**18 Mins.**

- ¼ C. extra-virgin olive oil
- 1 clove garlic, crushed
- 1 tbsp. Italian seasoning
- ½ tsp. paprika
- ½ lemon, sliced
- ¼ tsp. salt
- 1 lb. boneless, skinless chicken breasts
- 4 whole-grain pita breads
- 1 C. shredded lettuce
- ½ C. chopped tomatoes
- ¼ C. chopped red onion
- ¼ C. cucumber yogurt sauce

## Directions:

1. In a large resealable plastic bag, combine the olive oil, garlic, Italian seasoning, paprika, lemon, and salt. Add the chicken to the bag and secure shut. Vigorously shake until all the ingredients are combined. Set in the fridge for 2 hours to marinate.
2. When ready to cook, preheat the air fryer to 360°F.
3. Liberally spray the air fryer basket with olive oil mist. Remove the chicken from the bag and discard the leftover marinade. Place the chicken into the air fryer basket, allowing enough room between the chicken breasts to flip.
4. Cook for 10 minutes, flip, and cook another 8 minutes.
5. Remove the chicken from the air fryer basket when it has cooked (or the internal temperature of the chicken reaches 165°F). Let rest 5 minutes. Then thinly slice the chicken into strips.
6. Assemble the gyros by placing the pita bread on a flat surface and topping with chicken, lettuce, tomatoes, onion, and a drizzle of yogurt sauce.
7. Serve warm.

# Parmesan Chicken Fingers

## Ingredients:

- ½ C. flour
- 1 tsp. salt
- freshly ground black pepper
- 2 eggs, beaten
- ¾ C. seasoned panko breadcrumbs
- ¾ C. grated Parmesan cheese
- 8 chicken tenders (about 1 pound)
- OR
- 2 to 3 boneless, skinless chicken breasts, cut into strips
- vegetable oil
- marinara sauce

**Servings: 2**
**Cooking Time: 19 Mins.**

## Directions:

1. Set up a dredging station. Combine the flour, salt and pepper in a shallow dish. Place the beaten eggs in second shallow dish, and combine the panko breadcrumbs and Parmesan cheese in a third shallow dish.
2. Dredge the chicken tenders in the flour mixture. Then dip them into the egg, and finally place the chicken in the breadcrumb mixture. Press the coating onto both sides of the chicken tenders. Place the coated chicken tenders on a baking sheet until they are all coated. Spray both sides of the chicken fingers with vegetable oil.
3. Preheat the air fryer to 360°F.
4. Air-fry the chicken fingers in two batches. Transfer half the chicken fingers to the air fryer basket and air-fry for 9 minutes, turning the chicken over halfway through the cooking time. When the second batch of chicken fingers has finished cooking, return the first batch to the air fryer with the second batch and air-fry for one minute to heat everything through.
5. Serve immediately with marinara sauce, honey-mustard, ketchup or your favorite dipping sauce.

# Chicken Nuggets

## Ingredients:

- 1 lb. boneless, skinless chicken thighs, cut into 1-inch chunks
- ¾ tsp. salt
- ½ tsp. black pepper
- ½ tsp. garlic powder
- ½ tsp. onion powder
- ½ C. flour
- 2 eggs, beaten
- ½ C. panko breadcrumbs
- 3 tbsp. plain breadcrumbs
- oil for misting or cooking spray

*Servings: 20*
*Cooking Time:*
*14 Minutes*

## Directions:

1. In the bowl of a food processor, combine chicken, ½ tsp. salt, pepper, garlic powder, and onion powder. Process in short pulses until chicken is very finely chopped and well blended.
2. Place flour in one shallow dish and beaten eggs in another. In a third dish or plastic bag, mix together the panko crumbs, plain breadcrumbs, and ¼ tsp. salt.
3. Shape chicken mixture into small nuggets. Dip nuggets in flour, then eggs, then panko crumb mixture.
4. Spray nuggets on both sides with oil or cooking spray and place in air fryer basket in a single layer, close but not overlapping.
5. Cook at 360°F for 10minutes. Spray with oil and cook 4 minutes, until chicken is done and coating is golden brown.
6. Repeat step 5 to cook remaining nuggets.

# Chicken Chimichangas

## Ingredients:

- 2 C. cooked chicken, shredded
- 2 tbsp. chopped green chiles
- ½ tsp. oregano
- ½ tsp. cumin
- ½ tsp. onion powder
- ¼ tsp. garlic powder
- salt and pepper
- 8 flour tortillas (6- or 7-inch diameter)
- oil for misting or cooking spray
- Chimichanga Sauce
- 2 tbsp. butter
- 2 tbsp. flour
- 1 C. chicken broth
- ¼ C. light sour cream
- ¼ tsp. salt
- 2 oz. Pepper Jack or Monterey Jack cheese, shredded

*Servings: 4*
*Cooking Time:*
*10 Mins.*

## Directions:

1. Make the sauce by melting butter in a saucepan over medium-low heat. Stir in flour until smooth and slightly bubbly. Gradually add broth, stirring constantly until smooth. Cook and stir 1 minute, until the mixture slightly thickens. Remove from heat and stir in sour cream and salt. Set aside.

2. In a medium bowl, mix together the chicken, chiles, oregano, cumin, onion powder, garlic, salt, and pepper. Stir in 3 to 4 tbsp. of the sauce, using just enough to make the filling moist but not soupy.

3. Divide filling among the 8 tortillas. Place filling down the center of tortilla, stopping about 1 inch from edges. Fold one side of tortilla over filling, fold the two sides in, and then roll up. Mist all sides with oil or cooking spray.

4. Place chimichangas in air fryer basket seam side down. To fit more into the basket, you can stand them on their sides with the seams against the sides of the basket.

5. Cook at 360°F for 10 minutes or until heated through and crispy brown outside.

6. Add the shredded cheese to the remaining sauce. Stir over low heat, warming just until the cheese melts. Don't boil or sour cream may curdle.

7. Drizzle the sauce over the chimichangas.

# Honey Lemon Thyme Glazed Cornish Hen

## Ingredients:

- 1 (2-pound) Cornish game hen, split in half
- olive oil
- salt and freshly ground black pepper
- ¼ tsp. dried thyme
- ¼ C. honey
- 1 tbsp. lemon zest
- juice of 1 lemon
- 1½ tsp. chopped fresh thyme leaves
- ½ tsp. soy sauce
- freshly ground black pepper

*Servings: 2*
*Cooking Time:*
*20 Mins.*

## Directions:

1. Split the game hen in half by cutting down each side of the backbone and then cutting through the breast. Brush or spray both halves of the game hen with the olive oil and then season with the salt, pepper and dried thyme.
2. Preheat the air fryer to 390°F.
3. Place the game hen, skin side down, into the air fryer and air-fry for 5 minutes. Turn the hen halves over and air-fry for 10 minutes.
4. While the hen is cooking, combine the honey, lemon zest and juice, fresh thyme, soy sauce and pepper in a small bowl.
5. When the air fryer timer rings, brush the honey glaze onto the game hen and continue to air-fry for another 3 to 5 minutes, just until the hen is nicely glazed, browned and has an internal temperature of 165°F.
6. Let the hen rest for 5 minutes and serve warm.

# Chicken Flautas

## Ingredients:

- 6 tbsp. whipped cream cheese
- 1 C. shredded cooked chicken
- 6 tbsp. mild pico de gallo salsa
- ⅓ C. shredded Mexican cheese
- ½ tsp. taco seasoning
- Six 8-inch flour tortillas
- 2 C. shredded lettuce
- ½ C. guacamole

*Servings: 6*
*Cooking Time:*
*8 Mins.*

## Directions:

1. Preheat the air fryer to 370°F.
2. In a large bowl, mix the cream cheese, chicken, salsa, shredded cheese, and taco seasoning until well combined.
3. Lay the tortillas on a flat surface. Divide the cheese-and-chicken mixture into 6 equal portions; then place the mixture in the center of the tortillas, spreading evenly, leaving about 1 inch from the edge of the tortilla.
4. Spray the air fryer basket with olive oil spray. Roll up the flautas and place them edge side down into the basket. Lightly mist the top of the flautas with olive oil spray.
5. Repeat until the air fryer basket is full. You may need to cook these in batches, depending on the size of your air fryer.
6. Cook for 7 minutes, or until the outer edges are browned.
7. Remove from the air fryer basket and serve warm over a bed of shredded lettuce with guacamole on top.

# Chicken Cordon Bleu

## Ingredients:

- 2 boneless, skinless chicken breasts
- ¼ tsp. salt
- 2 tsp. Dijon mustard
- 2 oz. deli ham
- 2 oz. Swiss, fontina, or Gruyère cheese
- ⅓ C. all-purpose flour
- 1 egg
- ½ C. breadcrumbs

*Servings: 2*
*Cooking Time:*
*16 Mins.*

## Directions:

1. Pat the chicken breasts with a paper towel. Season the chicken with the salt. lb. the chicken breasts to 1½ inches thick. Create a pouch by slicing the side of each chicken breast. Spread 1 tsp. Dijon mustard inside the pouch of each chicken breast. Wrap a 1-oz. slice of ham around a 1-oz. slice of cheese and place into the pouch. Repeat with the remaining ham and cheese.
2. In a medium bowl, place the flour.
3. In a second bowl, whisk the egg.
4. In a third bowl, place the breadcrumbs.
5. Dredge the chicken in the flour and shake off the excess. Next, dip the chicken into the egg and then in the breadcrumbs. Set the chicken on a plate and repeat with the remaining chicken piece.
6. Preheat the air fryer to 360°F.
7. Place the chicken in the air fryer basket and spray liberally with cooking spray. Cook for 8 minutes, turn the chicken breasts over, and liberally spray with cooking spray again; cook another 6 minutes. Once golden brown, check for an internal temperature of 165°F.

# SANDWICHES AND BURGERS RECIPES

# Chicken Apple Brie Melt

## Ingredients:

- 3 5- to 6-oz. boneless skinless chicken breasts
- Vegetable oil spray
- 1½ tsp. Dried herbes de Provence
- 3 oz. Brie, rind removed, thinly sliced
- 6 Thin cored apple slices
- 3 French rolls (gluten-free, if a concern)
- 2 tbsp. Dijon mustard (gluten-free, if a concern)

*Servings: 3*
*Cooking Time:*
*13 Mins.*

## Directions:

1. Preheat the air fryer to 375°F.
2. Lightly coat all sides of the chicken breasts with vegetable oil spray. Sprinkle the breasts evenly with the herbes de Provence.
3. When the machine is at temperature, set the breasts in the basket and air-fry undisturbed for 10 minutes.
4. Top the chicken breasts with the apple slices, then the cheese. Air-fry undisturbed for 2 minutes, or until the cheese is melty and bubbling.
5. Use a nonstick-safe spatula and kitchen tongs, for balance, to transfer the breasts to a cutting board. Set the rolls in the basket and air-fry for 1 minute to warm through. (Putting them in the machine without splitting them keeps the insides very soft while the outside gets a little crunchy.)
6. Transfer the rolls to the cutting board. Split them open lengthwise, then spread 1 tsp. mustard on each cut side. Set a prepared chicken breast on the bottom of a roll and close with its top, repeating as necessary to make additional sandwiches. Serve warm.

# Inside Out Cheeseburgers

## Ingredients:

- ¾ lb. lean ground beef
- 3 tbsp. minced onion
- 4 tsp. ketchup
- 2 tsp. yellow mustard
- salt and freshly ground black pepper
- 4 slices of Cheddar cheese, broken into smaller pieces
- 8 hamburger dill pickle chips

*Servings: 2*
*Cooking Time:*
*20 Mins.*

## Directions:

1. Combine the ground beef, minced onion, ketchup, mustard, salt and pepper in a large bowl. Mix well to thoroughly combine the ingredients. Divide the meat into four equal portions.

2. To make the stuffed burgers, flatten each portion of meat into a thin patty. Place 4 pickle chips and half of the cheese onto the center of two of the patties, leaving a rim around the edge of the patty exposed. Place the remaining two patties on top of the first and press the meat together firmly, sealing the edges tightly. With the burgers on a flat surface, press the sides of the burger with the palm of your hand to create a straight edge. This will help keep the stuffing inside the burger while it cooks.

3. Preheat the air fryer to 370°F.

4. Place the burgers inside the air fryer basket and air-fry for 20 minutes, flipping the burgers over halfway through the cooking time.

5. Serve the cheeseburgers on buns with lettuce and tomato.

# Best-ever Roast Beef Sandwiches

## Ingredients:

*Servings: 6*
*Cooking Time:*
*30-50 Mins.*

- 2½ tsp. Olive oil
- 1½ tsp. Dried oregano
- 1½ tsp. Dried thyme
- 1½ tsp. Onion powder
- 1½ tsp. Table salt
- 1½ tsp. Ground black pepper
- 3 lb. Beef eye of round
- 6 Round soft rolls, such as Kaiser rolls or hamburger buns (gluten-free, if a concern), split open lengthwise
- ¾ C. Regular, low-fat, or fat-free mayonnaise (gluten-free, if a concern)
- 6 Romaine lettuce leaves, rinsed
- 6 Round tomato slices (¼ inch thick)

## Directions:

1. Preheat the air fryer to 350°F.
2. Mix the oil, oregano, thyme, onion powder, salt, and pepper in a small bowl. Spread this mixture all over the eye of round.
3. When the machine is at temperature, set the beef in the basket and air-fry for 30 to 50 minutes (the range depends on the size of the cut), turning the meat twice, until an instant-read meat thermometer inserted into the thickest piece of the meat registers 130°F for rare, 140°F for medium, or 150°F for well-done.
4. Use kitchen tongs to transfer the beef to a cutting board. Cool for 10 minutes. If serving now, carve into ⅛-inch-thick slices. Spread each roll with 2 tbsp. mayonnaise and divide the beef slices between the rolls. Top with a lettuce leaf and a tomato slice and serve. Or set the beef in a container, cover, and refrigerate for up to 3 days to make cold roast beef sandwiches anytime.

# Chili Cheese Dogs

## Ingredients:

- ¾ lb. Lean ground beef
- 1½ tbsp. Chile powder
- 1 C. plus 2 tbsp. Jarred sofrito
- 3 Hot dogs (gluten-free, if a concern)
- 3 Hot dog buns (gluten-free, if a concern), split open lengthwise
- 3 tbsp. Finely chopped scallion
- 9 tbsp. (a little more than 2 ounces) Shredded Cheddar cheese

## Directions:

1. Crumble the ground beef into a medium or large saucepan set over medium heat. Brown well, stirring often to break up the clumps. Add the chile powder and cook for 30 seconds, stirring the whole time. Stir in the sofrito and bring to a simmer. Reduce the heat to low and simmer, stirring occasionally, for 5 minutes. Keep warm.
2. Preheat the air fryer to 400°F.
3. When the machine is at temperature, put the hot dogs in the basket and air-fry undisturbed for 10 minutes, or until the hot dogs are bubbling and blistered, even a little crisp.
4. Use kitchen tongs to put the hot dogs in the buns. Top each with a ½ C. of the ground beef mixture, 1 tbsp. of the minced scallion, and 3 tbsp. of the cheese. (The scallion should go under the cheese so it superheats and wilts a bit.) Set the filled hot dog buns in the basket and air-fry undisturbed for 2 minutes, or until the cheese has melted.
5. Remove the basket from the machine. Cool the chili cheese dogs in the basket for 5 minutes before serving.

# Eggplant Parmesan Subs

## Ingredients:

- 4 Peeled eggplant slices (about ½ inch thick and 3 inches in diameter)
- Olive oil spray
- 2 tbsp. plus 2 tsp. Jarred pizza sauce, any variety except creamy
- ¼ C. (about ⅔ ounce) Finely grated Parmesan cheese
- 2 Small, long soft rolls, such as hero, hoagie, or Italian sub rolls (gluten-free, if a concern), split open lengthwise

*Servings: 2*
*Cooking Time:*
*13 Mins.*

## Directions:

1. Preheat the air fryer to 350°F.
2. When the machine is at temperature, coat both sides of the eggplant slices with olive oil spray. Set them in the basket in one layer and air-fry undisturbed for 10 minutes, until lightly browned and softened.
3. Increase the machine's temperature to 375°F (or 370°F, if that's the closest setting—unless the machine is already at 360°F, in which case leave it alone). Top each eggplant slice with 2 tsp. pizza sauce, then 1 tbsp. cheese. Air-fry undisturbed for 2 minutes, or until the cheese has melted.
4. Use a nonstick-safe spatula, and perhaps a flatware fork for balance, to transfer the eggplant slices cheese side up to a cutting board. Set the roll(s) cut side down in the basket in one layer (working in batches as necessary) and air-fry undisturbed for 1 minute, to toast the rolls a bit and warm them up. Set 2 eggplant slices in each warm roll.

# Chicken Gyros

## Ingredients:

- 4 4- to 5-oz. boneless skinless chicken thighs, trimmed of any fat blobs
- 2 tbsp. Lemon juice
- 2 tbsp. Red wine vinegar
- 2 tbsp. Olive oil
- 2 tsp. Dried oregano
- 2 tsp. Minced garlic
- 1 tsp. Table salt
- 1 tsp. Ground black pepper
- 4 Pita pockets (gluten-free, if a concern)
- ½ C. Chopped tomatoes
- ½ C. Bottled regular, low-fat, or fat-free ranch dressing (gluten-free, if a concern)

*Servings: 4*
*Cooking Time: 14 Mins.*

## Directions:

1. Mix the thighs, lemon juice, vinegar, oil, oregano, garlic, salt, and pepper in a zip-closed bag. Seal, gently massage the marinade into the meat through the plastic, and refrigerate for at least 2 hours or up to 6 hours. (Longer than that and the meat can turn rubbery.)

2. Set the plastic bag out on the counter (to make the contents a little less frigid). Preheat the air fryer to 375°F.

3. When the machine is at temperature, use kitchen tongs to place the thighs in the basket in one layer. Discard the marinade. Air-fry the chicken thighs undisturbed for 12 minutes, or until browned and an instant-read meat thermometer inserted into the thickest part of one thigh registers 165°F. You may need to air-fry the chicken 2 minutes longer if the machine's temperature is 360°F.

4. Use kitchen tongs to transfer the thighs to a cutting board. Cool for 5 minutes, then set one thigh in each of the pita pockets. Top each with 2 tbsp. chopped tomatoes and 2 tbsp. dressing. Serve warm.

# Lamb Burgers

## Ingredients:

- 1 lb. 2 oz. Ground lamb
- 3 tbsp. Crumbled feta
- 1 tsp. Minced garlic
- 1 tsp. Tomato paste
- ¾ tsp. Ground coriander
- ¾ tsp. Ground dried ginger
- Up to ⅛ tsp. Cayenne
- Up to a ⅛ tsp. Table salt (optional)
- 3 Kaiser rolls or hamburger buns (gluten-free, if a concern), split open

**Servings: 3**
**Cooking Time: 17 Mins.**

## Directions:

1. Preheat the air fryer to 375°F.
2. Gently mix the ground lamb, feta, garlic, tomato paste, coriander, ginger, cayenne, and salt (if using) in a bowl until well combined, trying to keep the bits of cheese intact. Form this mixture into two 5-inch patties for the small batch, three 5-inch patties for the medium, or four 5-inch patties for the large.
3. Set the patties in the basket in one layer and air-fry undisturbed for 16 minutes, or until an instant-read meat thermometer inserted into one burger registers 160°F. (The cheese is not an issue with the temperature probe in this recipe as it was for the Inside-Out Cheeseburgers, because the feta is so well mixed into the ground meat.)
4. Use a nonstick-safe spatula, and perhaps a flatware fork for balance, to transfer the burgers to a cutting board. Set the buns cut side down in the basket in one layer (working in batches as necessary) and air-fry undisturbed for 1 minute, to toast a bit and warm up. Serve the burgers warm in the buns.

# Philly Cheesesteak Sandwiches

## Ingredients:

- ¾ lb. Shaved beef
- 1 tbsp. Worcestershire sauce (gluten-free, if a concern)
- ¼ tsp. Garlic powder
- ¼ tsp. Mild paprika
- 6 tbsp. (1½ ounces) Frozen bell pepper strips (do not thaw)
- 2 slices, broken into rings Very thin yellow or white medium onion slice(s)
- 6 oz. (6 to 8 slices) Provolone cheese slices
- 3 Long soft rolls such as hero, hoagie, or Italian sub rolls, or hot dog buns (gluten-free, if a concern), split open lengthwise

## Directions:

1. Preheat the air fryer to 400°F.
2. When the machine is at temperature, spread the shaved beef in the basket, leaving a ½-inch perimeter around the meat for good air flow. Sprinkle the meat with the Worcestershire sauce, paprika, and garlic powder. Spread the peppers and onions on top of the meat.
3. Air-fry undisturbed for 6 minutes, or until cooked through. Set the cheese on top of the meat. Continue air-frying undisturbed for 3 minutes, or until the cheese has melted.
4. Use kitchen tongs to divide the meat and cheese layers in the basket between the rolls or buns. Serve hot.

# Chicken Spiedies

## Ingredients:

Servings: 3
Cooking Time:
12 Mins.

- 1¼ lb. Boneless skinless chicken thighs, trimmed of any fat blobs and cut into 2-inch pieces
- 3 tbsp. Red wine vinegar
- 2 tbsp. Olive oil
- 2 tbsp. Minced fresh mint leaves
- 2 tbsp. Minced fresh parsley leaves
- 2 tsp. Minced fresh dill fronds
- ¾ tsp. Fennel seeds
- ¾ tsp. Table salt
- Up to a ¼ tsp. Red pepper flakes
- 3 Long soft rolls, such as hero, hoagie, or Italian sub rolls (gluten-free, if a concern), split open lengthwise
- 4½ tbsp. Regular or low-fat mayonnaise (not fat-free; gluten-free, if a concern)
- 1½ tbsp. Distilled white vinegar
- 1½ tsp. Ground black pepper

## Directions:

1. Mix the chicken, vinegar, oil, mint, parsley, dill, fennel seeds, salt, and red pepper flakes in a zip-closed plastic bag. Seal, gently massage the marinade ingredients into the meat, and refrigerate for at least 2 hours or up to 6 hours. (Longer than that and the meat can turn rubbery.)
2. Set the plastic bag out on the counter (to make the contents a little less frigid). Preheat the air fryer to 400°F.
3. When the machine is at temperature, use kitchen tongs to set the chicken thighs in the basket (discard any remaining marinade) and air-fry undisturbed for 6 minutes. Turn the thighs over and continue air-frying undisturbed for 6 minutes more, until well browned, cooked through, and even a little crunchy.
4. Dump the contents of the basket onto a wire rack and cool for 2 or 3 minutes. Divide the chicken evenly between the rolls. Whisk the mayonnaise, vinegar, and black pepper in a small bowl until smooth. Drizzle this sauce over the chicken pieces in the rolls.

# APPETIZERS AND SNACKS

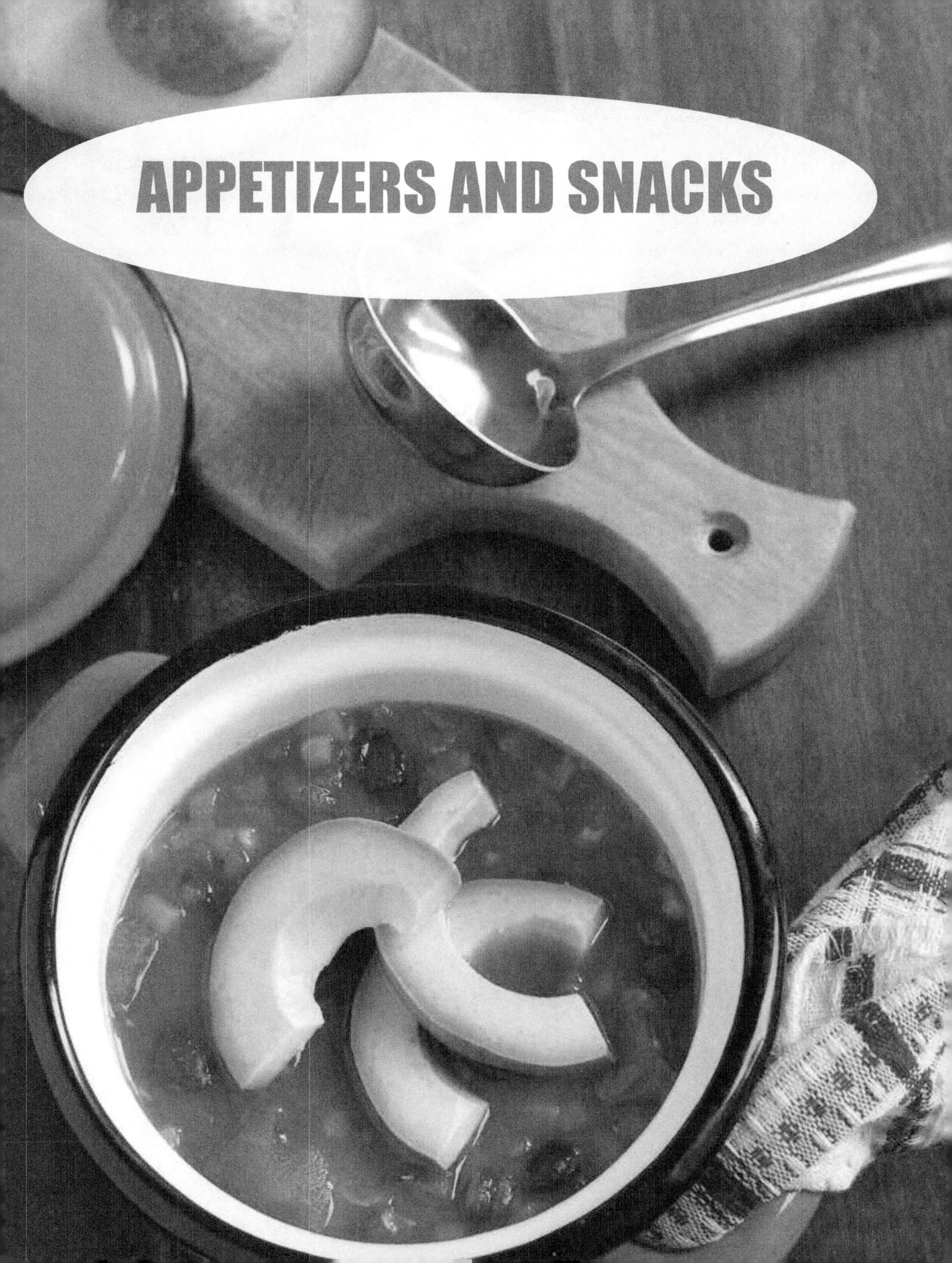

# Potato Chips

## Ingredients:

- 2 medium potatoes
- 2 tsp. extra-light olive oil
- oil for misting or cooking spray
- salt and pepper

*Servings: 2*
*Cooking Time:*
*15 Mins.*

## Directions:

1. Peel the potatoes.
2. Using a mandoline or paring knife, shave potatoes into thin slices, dropping them into a bowl of water as you cut them.
3. Dry potatoes as thoroughly as possible with paper towels or a clean dish towel. Toss potato slices with the oil to coat completely.
4. Spray air fryer basket with cooking spray and add potato slices.
5. Stir and separate with a fork.
6. Cook 390°F for 5minutes. Stir and separate potato slices. Cook 5 more minutes. Stir and separate potatoes again. Cook another 5minutes.
7. Season to taste.

# Fried Goat Cheese

## Ingredients:

- 7 oz. 1- to 1½-inch-diameter goat cheese log
- 2 Large egg(s)
- 1¾ C. Plain dried bread crumbs (gluten-free, if a concern)
- Vegetable oil spray

## Directions:

1. Slice the goat cheese log into ½-inch-thick rounds. Set these flat on a small cutting board, a small baking sheet, or a large plate. Freeze uncovered for 30 minutes.
2. Preheat the air fryer to 400°F.
3. Set up and fill two shallow soup plates or small pie plates on your counter: one in which you whisk the egg(s) until uniform and the other for the bread crumbs.
4. Take the goat cheese rounds out of the freezer. With clean, dry hands, dip one round in the egg(s) to coat it on all sides. Let the excess egg slip back into the rest, then dredge the round in the bread crumbs, turning it to coat all sides, even the edges. Repeat this process—egg, then bread crumbs—for a second coating. Coat both sides of the round and its edges with vegetable oil spray, then set it aside. Continue double-dipping, double-dredging, and spraying the remaining rounds.
5. Place the rounds in one layer in the basket. Air-fry undisturbed for 4 minutes, or until lightly browned and crunchy. Do not overcook. Some of the goat cheese may break through the crust. A few little breaks are fine but stop the cooking before the coating reaches structural failure.
6. Remove the basket from the machine and set aside for 3 minutes. Use a nonstick-safe spatula, and maybe a flatware fork for balance, to transfer the rounds to a wire rack. Cool for 5 minutes more before serving.

# Antipasto-stuffed Cherry Tomatoes

## Ingredients:

- 12 Large cherry tomatoes, preferably Campari tomatoes (about 1½ oz. each and the size of golf balls)
- ½ C. Seasoned Italian-style dried bread crumbs (gluten-free, if a concern)
- ¼ C. (about ¾ ounce) Finely grated Parmesan cheese
- ¼ C. Finely chopped pitted black olives
- ¼ C. Finely chopped marinated artichoke hearts
- 2 tbsp. Marinade from the artichokes
- 4 Sun-dried tomatoes (dry, not packed in oil), finely chopped
- Olive oil spray

**Servings: 12**
**Cooking Time: 9 Mins.**

## Directions:

1. Preheat the air fryer to 400°F.
2. Cut the top off of each fresh tomato, exposing the seeds and pulp. (The tops can be saved for a snack, sprinkled with some kosher salt, to tide you over while the stuffed tomatoes cook.) Cut a very small slice off the bottom of each tomato (no cutting into the pulp) so it will stand up flat on your work surface. Use a melon baller to remove and discard the seeds and pulp from each tomato.
3. Mix the bread crumbs, cheese, olives, artichoke hearts, marinade, and sun-dried tomatoes in a bowl until well combined. Stuff this mixture into each prepared tomato, about 1½ tbsp. in each. Generously coat the tops of the tomatoes with olive oil spray.
4. Set the tomatoes stuffing side up in the basket. Air-fry undisturbed for 9 minutes, or until the stuffing has browned a bit and the tomatoes are blistered in places.
5. Remove the basket and cool the tomatoes in it for 5 minutes. Then use kitchen tongs to gently transfer the tomatoes to a serving platter.

# Blooming Onion

## Ingredients:

- 1 large Vidalia onion, peeled
- 2 eggs
- ½ C. milk
- 1 C. flour
- 1 tsp. salt
- ½ tsp. freshly ground black pepper
- ¼ tsp. ground cayenne pepper
- ½ tsp. paprika
- ½ tsp. garlic powder
- Dipping Sauce:
- ½ C. mayonnaise
- ½ C. ketchup
- 1 tsp. Worcestershire sauce
- ½ tsp. ground cayenne pepper
- ½ tsp. paprika
- ½ tsp. onion powder

**Servings: 4**
**Cooking Time: 25 Mins.**

## Directions:

1. Cut off the top inch of the onion, leaving the root end of the onion intact. Place the now flat, stem end of the onion down on a cutting board with the root end facing up. Make 16 slices around the onion, starting with your knife tip ½-inch away from the root so that you never slice through the root. Begin by making slices at 12, 3, 6 and 9 o'clock around the onion. Then make three slices down the onion in between each of the original four slices. Turn the onion over, gently separate the onion petals, and remove the loose pieces of onion in the center.

2. Combine the eggs and milk in a bowl. In a second bowl, combine the flour, salt, black pepper, cayenne pepper, paprika, and garlic powder.

3. Preheat the air fryer to 350°F.

4. Place the onion cut side up into a third empty bowl. Sprinkle the flour mixture all over the onion to cover it and get in between the onion petals. Turn the onion over to carefully shake off the excess flour and then transfer the onion to the empty flour bowl, again cut side up.

5. Pour the egg mixture all over the onion to cover all the flour. Let it soak for a minute in the mixture. Carefully remove the onion, tipping it upside down to drain off any excess egg, and transfer it to the empty egg bowl, again cut side up.

6. Finally, sprinkle the flour mixture over the onion a second time, making sure the onion is well coated and all the petals have the seasoned flour mixture on them. Carefully turn the onion over, shake off any excess flour and transfer it to a plate or baking sheet. Spray the onion generously with vegetable oil.

7. Transfer the onion, cut side up to the air fryer basket and air-fry for 25 minutes. The onion petals will open more fully as it cooks, so spray with more vegetable oil at least twice during the cooking time.

8. While the onion is cooking, make the dipping sauce by combining all the dip ingredients and mixing well. Serve the Blooming Onion as soon as it comes out of the air fryer with dipping sauce on the side.

# Mozzarella En Carrozza With Puttanesca Sauce

## Ingredients:

- Puttanesca Sauce
- 2 tsp. olive oil
- 1 anchovy, chopped (optional)
- 2 cloves garlic, minced
- 1 (14-oz.) can petite diced tomatoes
- ½ C. chicken stock or water
- ⅓ C. Kalamata olives, chopped
- 2 tbsp. capers
- ½ tsp. dried oregano
- ¼ tsp. crushed red pepper flakes
- salt and freshly ground black pepper

- 1 tbsp. fresh parsley, chopped
- 8 slices of thinly sliced white bread (Pepperidge Farm®)
- 8 oz. mozzarella cheese, cut into ¼-inch slices
- ½ C. all-purpose flour
- 3 eggs, beaten
- 1½ C. seasoned panko breadcrumbs
- ½ tsp. garlic powder
- ½ tsp. salt
- freshly ground black pepper
- olive oil, in a spray bottle

***Servings: 6***
***Cooking Time: 8 Mins.***

## Directions:

1. Start by making the puttanesca sauce. Heat the olive oil in a medium saucepan on the stovetop. Add the anchovies (if using, and I really think you should!) and garlic and sauté for 3 minutes, or until the anchovies have "melted" into the oil. Add the tomatoes, chicken stock, olives, capers, oregano and crushed red pepper flakes and simmer the sauce for 20 minutes. Season with salt and freshly ground black pepper and stir in the fresh parsley.

2. Cut the crusts off the slices of bread. Place four slices of the bread on a cutting board. Divide the cheese between the four slices of bread. Top the cheese with the remaining four slices of bread to make little sandwiches and cut each sandwich into 4 triangles.

3. Set up a dredging station using three shallow dishes. Place the flour in the first shallow dish, the eggs in the second dish and in the third dish, combine the panko breadcrumbs, garlic powder, salt and black pepper. Dredge each little triangle in the flour first (you might think this is redundant, but it helps to get the coating to adhere to the edges of the sandwiches) and then dip them into the egg, making sure both the sides and the edges are coated. Let the excess egg drip off and then press the triangles into the breadcrumb mixture, pressing the crumbs on with your hands so they adhere. Place the coated triangles in the freezer for 2 hours, until the cheese is frozen.

4. Preheat the air fryer to 390°F. Spray all sides of the mozzarella triangles with oil and transfer a single layer of triangles to the air fryer basket. Air-fry in batches at 390°F for 5 minutes. Turn the triangles over and air-fry for an additional 3 minutes.

5. Serve mozzarella triangles immediately with the warm puttanesca sauce.

# Pork Pot Stickers With Yum Yum Sauce

## Ingredients:

- 1 lb. ground pork
- 2 C. shredded green cabbage
- ¼ C. shredded carrot
- ½ C. finely chopped water chestnuts
- 2 tsp. minced fresh ginger
- ¼ C. hoisin sauce
- 2 tbsp. soy sauce
- 1 tbsp. sesame oil
- freshly ground black pepper
- 3 scallions, minced
- 48 round dumpling wrappers (or wonton wrappers with the corners cut off to make them round)
- 1 tbsp. vegetable oil
- soy sauce, for serving
- Yum Yum Sauce:
- 1½ C. mayonnaise
- 2 tbsp. sugar
- 3 tbsp. rice vinegar
- 1 tsp. soy sauce
- 2 tbsp. ketchup
- 1½ tsp. paprika
- ¼ tsp. ground cayenne pepper
- ¼ tsp. garlic powder

**Servings: 48**
**Cooking Time: 8 Mins.**

## Directions:

1. Preheat a large sauté pan over medium-high heat. Add the ground pork and brown for a few minutes. Remove the cooked pork to a bowl using a slotted spoon and discard the fat from the pan. Return the cooked pork to the sauté pan and add the cabbage, carrots and water chestnuts. Sauté for a minute and then add the fresh ginger, hoisin sauce, soy sauce, sesame oil, and freshly ground black pepper. Sauté for a few more minutes, just until cabbage and carrots are soft. Then stir in the scallions and transfer the pork filling to a bowl to cool.

2. Make the pot stickers in batches of 1 Place 12 dumpling wrappers on a flat surface. Brush a little water around the perimeter of the wrappers. Place a rounded tsp. of the filling into the center of each wrapper. Fold the wrapper over the filling, bringing the edges together to form a half moon, sealing the edges shut. Brush a little more water on the top surface of the sealed edge of the pot sticker. Make pleats in the dough around the sealed edge by pinching the dough and folding the edge over on itself. You should have about 5 to 6 pleats in the dough. Repeat this three times until you have 48 pot stickers. Freeze the pot stickers for 2 hours (or as long as 3 weeks in an airtight container).

3. Preheat the air fryer to 400°F.

4. Air-fry the pot stickers in batches of 16. Brush or spray the pot stickers with vegetable oil just before putting them in the air fryer basket. Air-fry for 8 minutes, turning the pot stickers once or twice during the cooking process.

5. While the pot stickers are cooking, combine all the ingredients for the Yum Yum sauce in a bowl. Serve the pot stickers warm with the Yum Yum sauce and soy sauce for dipping.

# VEGETARIANS RECIPES

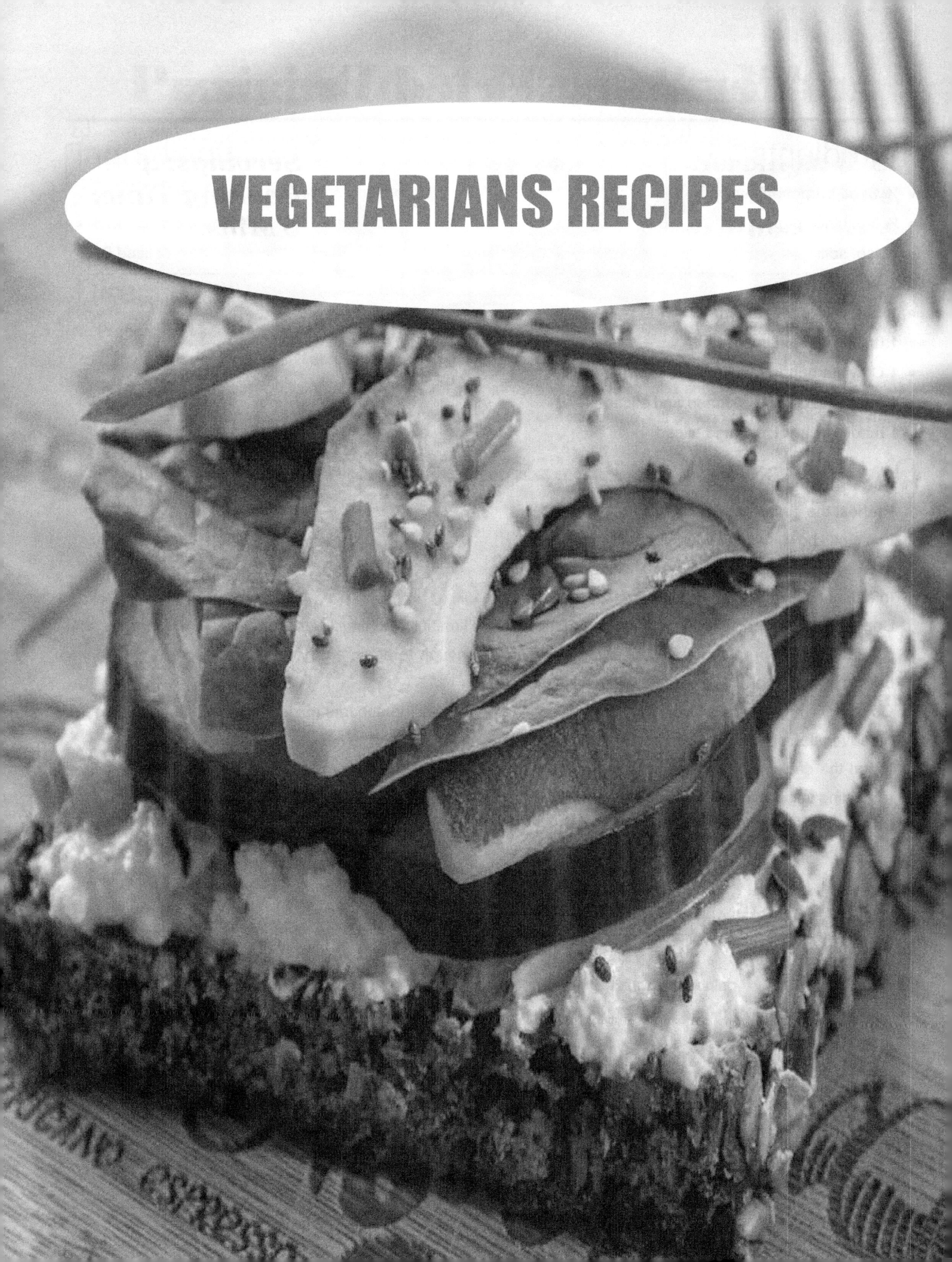

# Parmesan Portobello Mushroom Caps

## Ingredients:

- ¼ C. flour*
- 1 egg, lightly beaten
- 1 C. seasoned breadcrumbs*
- 2 large portobello mushroom caps, stems and gills removed
- olive oil, in a spray bottle
- ½ C. tomato sauce
- ¾ C. grated mozzarella cheese
- 1 tbsp. grated Parmesan cheese
- 1 tbsp. chopped fresh basil or parsley

**Servings: 2**
**Cooking Time: 14 Mins.**

## Directions:

1. Set up a dredging station with three shallow dishes. Place the flour in the first shallow dish, egg in the second dish and breadcrumbs in the last dish. Dredge the mushrooms in flour, then dip them into the egg and finally press them into the breadcrumbs to coat on all sides. Spray both sides of the coated mushrooms with olive oil.
2. Preheat the air fryer to 400°F.
3. Air-fry the mushrooms at 400°F for 10 minutes, turning them over halfway through the cooking process.
4. Fill the underside of the mushrooms with the tomato sauce and then top the sauce with the mozzarella and Parmesan cheeses. Reset the air fryer temperature to 350°F and air-fry for an additional 4 minutes, until the cheese has melted and is slightly browned.
5. Serve the mushrooms with pasta tossed with tomato sauce and garnish with some chopped fresh basil or parsley.

# Vegetable Couscous

## Ingredients:

- 4 oz. white mushrooms, sliced
- ½ medium green bell pepper, julienned
- 1 C. cubed zucchini
- ¼ small onion, slivered
- 1 stalk celery, thinly sliced
- ¼ tsp. ground coriander
- ¼ tsp. ground cumin
- salt and pepper
- 1 tbsp. olive oil
- Couscous
- ¾ C. uncooked couscous
- 1 C. vegetable broth or water
- ½ tsp. salt (omit if using salted broth)

*Servings: 4*
*Cooking Time:*
*10 Mins.*

## Directions:

1. Combine all vegetables in large bowl. Sprinkle with coriander, cumin, and salt and pepper to taste. Stir well, add olive oil, and stir again to coat vegetables evenly.
2. Place vegetables in air fryer basket and cook at 390°F for 5minutes. Stir and cook for 5 more minutes, until tender.
3. While vegetables are cooking, prepare the couscous: Place broth or water and salt in large saucepan. Heat to boiling, stir in couscous, cover, and remove from heat.
4. Let couscous sit for 5minutes, stir in cooked vegetables, and serve hot.

# Falafels

## Ingredients:

- 1 pouch falafel mix
- 2–3 tbsp. plain breadcrumbs
- oil for misting or cooking spray

**Servings: 12**
**Cooking Time:**
**10 Mins.**

## Directions:

1. Prepare falafel mix according to package directions.
2. Preheat air fryer to 390°F.
3. Place breadcrumbs in shallow dish or on wax paper.
4. Shape falafel mixture into 12 balls and flatten slightly. Roll in breadcrumbs to coat all sides and mist with oil or cooking spray.
5. Place falafels in air fryer basket in single layer and cook for 5minutes. Shake basket, and continue cooking for 5minutes, until they brown and are crispy.

# Veggie Fried Rice

## Ingredients:

- 1 C. cooked brown rice
- ⅓ C. chopped onion
- ½ C. chopped carrots
- ½ C. chopped bell peppers
- ½ C. chopped broccoli florets
- 3 tbsp. low-sodium soy sauce
- 1 tbsp. sesame oil
- 1 tsp. ground ginger
- 1 tsp. ground garlic powder
- ½ tsp. black pepper
- ⅛ tsp. salt
- 2 large eggs

*Servings: 4*
*Cooking Time:*
*25 Mins.*

## Directions:

1. Preheat the air fryer to 370°F.
2. In a large bowl, mix together the brown rice, onions, carrots, bell pepper, and broccoli.
3. In a small bowl, whisk together the soy sauce, sesame oil, ginger, garlic powder, pepper, salt, and eggs.
4. Pour the egg mixture into the rice and vegetable mixture and mix together.
5. Liberally spray a 7-inch springform pan (or compatible air fryer dish) with olive oil. Add the rice mixture to the pan and cover with aluminum foil.
6. Place a metal trivet into the air fryer basket and set the pan on top. Cook for 15 minutes. Carefully remove the pan from basket, discard the foil, and mix the rice. Return the rice to the air fryer basket, turning down the temperature to 350°F and cooking another 10 minutes.
7. Remove and let cool 5 minutes. Serve warm.

# Corn And Pepper Jack Chile Rellenos With Roasted Tomato Sauce

## Ingredients:

- 3 Poblano peppers
- 1 C. all-purpose flour*
- salt and freshly ground black pepper
- 2 eggs, lightly beaten
- 1 C. plain breadcrumbs*
- olive oil, in a spray bottle
- Sauce
- 2 C. cherry tomatoes
- 1 Jalapeño pepper, halved and seeded
- 1 clove garlic
- ¼ red onion, broken into large pieces
- 1 tbsp. olive oil
- salt, to taste
- 2 tbsp. chopped fresh cilantro
- Filling
- olive oil
- ¼ red onion, finely chopped
- 1 tsp. minced garlic
- 1 C. corn kernels, fresh or frozen
- 2 C. grated pepper jack cheese

***Servings: 3
Cooking Time:
30 Mins.***

## Directions:

1. Start by roasting the peppers. Preheat the air fryer to 400°F. Place the peppers into the air fryer basket and air-fry at 400°F for 10 minutes, turning them over halfway through the cooking time. Remove the peppers from the basket and cover loosely with foil.

2. While the peppers are cooling, make the roasted tomato sauce. Place all sauce Ingredients except for the cilantro into the air fryer basket and air-fry at 400°F for 10 minutes, shaking the basket once or twice. When the sauce Ingredients have finished air-frying, transfer everything to a blender or food processor and blend or process to a smooth sauce, adding a little warm water to get the desired consistency. Season to taste with salt, add the cilantro and set aside.

3. While the sauce Ingredients are cooking in the air fryer, make the filling. Heat a skillet on the stovetop over medium heat. Add the olive oil and sauté the red onion and garlic for 4 to 5 minutes. Transfer the onion and garlic to a bowl, stir in the corn and cheese, and set aside.

4. Set up a dredging station with three shallow dishes. Place the flour, seasoned with salt and pepper, in the first shallow dish. Place the eggs in the second dish, and fill the third shallow dish with the breadcrumbs. When the peppers have cooled, carefully slice into one side of the pepper to create an opening. Pull the seeds out of the peppers and peel away the skins, trying not to tear the pepper. Fill each pepper with some of the corn and cheese filling and close the pepper up again by folding one side of the opening over the other. Carefully roll each pepper in the seasoned flour, then into the egg and finally into the breadcrumbs to coat on all sides, trying not to let the pepper fall open. Spray the peppers on all sides with a little olive oil.

5. Air-fry two peppers at a time at 350°F for 6 minutes. Turn the peppers over and air-fry for another 4 minutes. Serve the peppers warm on a bed of the roasted tomato sauce.

# VEGETABLE SIDE DISHES RECIPES

# Roasted Fennel Salad

## Ingredients:

Servings: 3
Cooking Time:
20 Mins.

- 3 C. (about ¾ pound) Trimmed fennel (see the headnote), roughly chopped
- 1½ tbsp. Olive oil
- ¼ tsp. Table salt
- ¼ tsp. Ground black pepper
- 1½ tbsp. White balsamic vinegar (see here)

## Directions:

1. Preheat the air fryer to 400°F.
2. Toss the fennel, olive oil, salt, and pepper in a large bowl until the fennel is well coated in the oil.
3. When the machine is at temperature, pour the fennel into the basket, spreading it out into as close to one layer as possible. Air-fry for 20 minutes, tossing and rearranging the fennel pieces twice so that any covered or touching parts get exposed to the air currents, until golden at the edges and softened.
4. Pour the fennel into a serving bowl. Add the vinegar while hot. Toss well, then cool a couple of minutes before serving. Or serve at room temperature.

# Roasted Heirloom Carrots With Orange And Thyme

## Ingredients:

Servings: 2
Cooking Time:
12 Mins.

- 10 to 12 heirloom or rainbow carrots (about 1 pound), scrubbed but not peeled
- 1 tsp. olive oil
- salt and freshly ground black pepper
- 1 tbsp. butter
- 1 tsp. fresh orange zest
- 1 tsp. chopped fresh thyme

## Directions:

1. Preheat the air fryer to 400°F.
2. Scrub the carrots and halve them lengthwise. Toss them in the olive oil, season with salt and freshly ground black pepper and transfer to the air fryer.
3. Air-fry at 400°F for 12 minutes, shaking the basket every once in a while to rotate the carrots as they cook.
4. As soon as the carrots have finished cooking, add the butter, orange zest and thyme and toss all the ingredients together in the air fryer basket to melt the butter and coat evenly. Serve warm.

# Zucchini Fries

## Ingredients:

- 1 large Zucchini
- ½ C. All-purpose flour or tapioca flour
- 2 Large egg(s), well beaten
- 1 C. Seasoned Italian-style dried bread crumbs (gluten-free, if a concern)
- Olive oil spray

*Servings: 3*
*Cooking Time: 12 Mins.*

## Directions:

1. Preheat the air fryer to 400°F.
2. Trim the zucchini into a long rectangular block, taking off the ends and four "sides" to make this shape. Cut the block lengthwise into ½-inch-thick slices. Lay these slices flat and cut in half widthwise. Slice each of these pieces into ½-inch-thick batons.
3. Set up and fill three shallow soup plates or small pie plates on your counter: one for the flour, one for the beaten egg(s), and one for the bread crumbs.
4. Set a zucchini baton in the flour and turn it several times to coat all sides. Gently shake off any excess flour, then dip it in the egg(s), turning it to coat. Let any excess egg slip back into the rest, then set the baton in the bread crumbs and turn it several times, pressing gently to coat all sides, even the ends. Set aside on a cutting board and continue coating the remainder of the batons in the same way.
5. Lightly coat the batons on all sides with olive oil spray. Set them in two flat layers in the basket, the top layer at a 90-degree angle to the bottom one, with a little air space between the batons in each layer. In the end, the whole thing will look like a crosshatch pattern. Air-fry undisturbed for 6 minutes.
6. Use kitchen tongs to gently rearrange the batons so that any covered parts are now uncovered. The batons no longer need to be in a crosshatch pattern. Continue air-frying undisturbed for 6 minutes, or until lightly browned and crisp.
7. Gently pour the contents of the basket onto a wire rack. Spread the batons out and cool for only a minute or two before serving.

# Sweet Potato Fries

## Ingredients:

- 2 lb. sweet potatoes
- 1 tsp. dried marjoram
- 2 tsp. olive oil
- sea salt

*Servings: 4*
*Cooking Time:*
*30 Mins.*

## Directions:

1. Peel and cut the potatoes into ¼-inch sticks, 4 to 5 inches long.
2. In a sealable plastic bag or bowl with lid, toss sweet potatoes with marjoram and olive oil. Rub seasonings in to coat well.
3. Pour sweet potatoes into air fryer basket and cook at 390°F for approximately 30 minutes, until cooked through with some brown spots on edges.
4. Season to taste with sea salt.

# Cheesy Texas Toast

## Ingredients:

- 2 1-inch-thick slice(s) Italian bread (each about 4 inches across)
- 4 tsp. Softened butter
- 2 tsp. Minced garlic
- ¼ C. (about ¾ ounce) Finely grated Parmesan cheese

*Servings: 2*
*Cooking Time:*
*4 Mins.*

## Directions:

1. Preheat the air fryer to 400°F.
2. Spread one side of a slice of bread with 2 tsp. butter. Sprinkle with 1 tsp. minced garlic, followed by 2 tbsp. grated cheese. Repeat this process if you're making one or more additional toasts.
3. When the machine is at temperature, put the bread slice(s) cheese side up in the basket (with as much air space between them as possible if you're making more than one). Air-fry undisturbed for 4 minutes, or until browned and crunchy.
4. Use a nonstick-safe spatula to transfer the toasts cheese side up to a wire rack. Cool for 5 minutes before serving.

# Broccoli Tots

## Ingredients:

- 2 C. broccoli florets (about ½ lb. broccoli crowns)
- 1 egg, beaten
- ⅛ tsp. onion powder
- ¼ tsp. salt
- ⅛ tsp. pepper
- 2 tbsp. grated Parmesan cheese
- ¼ C. panko breadcrumbs
- oil for misting

## Directions:

1. Steam broccoli for 2minutes. Rinse in cold water, drain well, and chop finely.
2. In a large bowl, mix broccoli with all other ingredients except the oil.
3. Scoop out small portions of mixture and shape into 24 tots. Lay them on a cookie sheet or wax paper as you work.
4. Spray tots with oil and place in air fryer basket in single layer.
5. Cook at 390°F for 5minutes. Shake basket and spray with oil again. Cook 5minutes longer or until browned and crispy.

# Crispy Noodle Salad

## Ingredients:

- 6 oz. Fresh Chinese-style stir-fry or lo mein wheat noodles
- 1½ tbsp. Cornstarch
- ¾ C. Chopped stemmed and cored red bell pepper
- 2 Medium scallion(s), trimmed and thinly sliced
- 2 tsp. Sambal oelek or other pulpy hot red pepper sauce (see here)
- 2 tsp. Thai sweet chili sauce or red ketchup-like chili sauce, such as Heinz
- 2 tsp. Regular or low-sodium soy sauce or tamari sauce
- 2 tsp. Unseasoned rice vinegar (see here)
- 1 tbsp. White or black sesame seeds

*Servings: 3*
*Cooking Time:*
*22 Mins.*

## Directions:

1. Bring a large saucepan of water to a boil over high heat. Add the noodles and boil for 2 minutes. Drain in a colander set in the sink. Rinse several times with cold water, shaking the colander to drain the noodles very well. Spread the noodles out on a large cutting board and air-dry for 10 minutes.
2. Preheat the air fryer to 400°F.
3. Toss the noodles in a bowl with the cornstarch until well coated. Spread them out across the entire basket (although they will be touching and overlapping a bit). Air-fry for 6 minutes, then turn the solid mass of noodles over as one piece. If it cracks in half or smaller pieces, just fit these back together after turning. Continue air-frying for 6 minutes, or until golden brown and crisp.
4. As the noodles cook, stir the bell pepper, scallion(s), sambal oelek, red chili sauce, soy sauce, vinegar, and sesame seeds in a serving bowl until well combined.
5. Turn the basket of noodles out onto a cutting board and cool for a minute or two. Break the mass of noodles into individual noodles and/or small chunks and add to the dressing in the serving bowl. Toss well to serve.

# Roasted Ratatouille Vegetables

## Ingredients:

- 1 baby or Japanese eggplant, cut into 1½-inch cubes
- 1 red pepper, cut into 1-inch chunks
- 1 yellow pepper, cut into 1-inch chunks
- 1 zucchini, cut into 1-inch chunks
- 1 clove garlic, minced
- ½ tsp. dried basil
- 1 tbsp. olive oil
- salt and freshly ground black pepper
- ¼ C. sliced sun-dried tomatoes in oil
- 2 tbsp. chopped fresh basil

**Servings: 2**
**Cooking Time: 15 Mins.**

## Directions:

1. Preheat the air fryer to 400°F.
2. Toss the eggplant, peppers and zucchini with the garlic, dried basil, olive oil, salt and freshly ground black pepper.
3. Air-fry the vegetables at 400°F for 15 minutes, shaking the basket a few times during the cooking process to redistribute the ingredients.
4. As soon as the vegetables are tender, toss them with the sliced sun-dried tomatoes and fresh basil and serve.

Printed in Great Britain
by Amazon

32380702R00064